LETTERS TO MY GRANDDAUGHTERS

LETTERS TO MY GRANDDAUGHTERS

*Insights and inspiration
for a life journey*

Linda Abbott Trapp

Cover photo, author. Author photo, josef kandoll w.

Copyright © 2007 by Linda Abbott Trapp.

| ISBN 10: | Softcover | 1-4257-3941-5 |
| ISBN 13: | Softcover | 978-1-4257-3941-6 |

This book first printed in the United States of America.
Second printing, Korea

CONTENTS

Letters to My Granddaughters

Insights and inspiration for a life journey
filled with beauty, joy, contentment, and impact

Each letter is complete with workbook questions for
application to real-life situations

*dedicated to Kesla and Kylie: may the love in these
letters encourage, comfort, and strengthen you in
your travels through life*

Introduction/Acknowledgments

Generativity—it's not a particularly compelling word, but the impulse is unavoidable. At some time in the late mid-career years, adults begin to feel a strong need to pass on what they have learned, to prevent others from having to repeat their mistakes. For me, the two major life arenas, love and work, were so full of change and demand that I almost missed the early warning signs of the generativity impulse. Then, my husband had a "cardiac incident", and we were propelled into an earlier-than-expected retirement, moving to a more affordable life in Mexico. There, the impulse took form and became stronger.

For years, participants in my seminars on communication, conflict resolution, mutual respect, and similar workplace topics had asked, "Where's the book?" I understood that the principles and techniques we were discussing had applicability far beyond the workplace, and knew they wanted a tool with which to open discussions of these topics with those they loved. Constant travel and family and community needs were my excuse for not writing. Now, in semi-retirement, that excuse was gone.

At the same time, my two oldest grandchildren were becoming young women, and facing considerable changes in their own lives. So, with them in mind, I began to write the things that people in my seminars had asked for, an instruction manual of sorts, bringing the insights of psychology, the guidance of wisdom borrowed from many cultures, and the experiences of a full life to bear on the questions that inevitably arise in trying to make sense of life. My hope is that the reader will be led to his or her own truths, and further, that these letters will ease the path and heighten the excitement and joy that is there for us all. Just ponder the essays, or use the workbook questions as a stimulus for your own search.

The process of getting it all down was inspired, of course, by the good people in the seminars, and the illustrations for many of the stories included are inspired by the family I'm so fortunate to have. The Puerto Vallarta Writers Group, particularly Daniel Grippo and Sally Conley, were extremely supportive and helpful. Writer Bob Rossier provided practical advice as well as much-needed encouragement. Bob

Brothers of the City of Stockton was a most appreciated cheerleader, and provided further insights into client needs that the book addresses. To them, and to the wise and thoughtful leaders whose ideas are quoted throughout the book, my heartfelt gratitude. To you, the reader, my thanks, and my hope that this book will ease your path and bring you joy.

Linda Abbott Trapp, PhD
Puerto Vallarta, Mexico 2006

Chapter 1

Some Things That Really Matter

Joy

- The Nature of Joy, and how to align with it
- Joy is available in good times and bad
- You can awake to more joy in your life; more intensely, and more often
- We have to let go of our self-obsession to experience joy
- Here are the simple first steps to more joy

Once in a very great while, more often if you're incredibly lucky, joy will drop into your life. It may be a simple thing, such as seeing an exceptionally beautiful flower, or it might be one of life's peak experiences, like the birth of a child, that triggers the emotion of joy. Whatever brings it on, take immediate action. Notice it, stop everything else. Breathe it in, listen to it, touch it, taste it, smell it, revel in it, roll around in it, suspend time and ignore everyone else. This is too important for manners, for civilized, polite behavior. Joy is elemental, real, and rare.

When Kesla, the first grandchild, came into this world, I was in San Francisco, attending a meeting of a group I had worked very hard to be welcomed into. We were all so self-important, so potentially powerful, and our meetings so very informative and elegant, that they must have thought I was stupid or crazy, or both, to abandon them in a rush, shouting over my shoulder, "She's just been born!" I ran for the parking lot, raced to Fresno, dashed into the hospital room, and held her for the first time. I remember promising, "Honey, when you're ten, we're going to Paris!", although I had never had that thought before, and don't remember why I said it. Probably it was some kind of altered mental state, induced by joy.

Years later, that same joy came back to visit, although it didn't look that way at first. My daughter Heather had a hard time when Carson was born—back labor, they said. She was so exhausted, so tired from all the hours of pain. Her husband

Mark was wonderful to watch with his newborn son—a giant of a man so tender, so loving and so clearly awed. But the best moment for me was watching when he first handed the baby, a few minutes old, to Heather. Her outstretched arms and tears of joy are inscribed forever on my brain.

Sometimes the grace of joy comes in time to heal a hurt or keep us from making a mistake. When we first moved into an unfinished house in Mexico, we suffered through the learning process of construction in a different culture. There were times I really hated it and regretted our decision. One day, after several days without hot water and other comforts, I was just fed up! I stormed from the house in a rage, heading for the street, ready to just keep going. Just then, a flock of 50 or 60 beautiful, chirping, wild parakeets flew just over my head and settled in the tree across the street. I looked up and said "OK, God, I get it; it's not about the hot water".

It's not always the big stuff that brings joy, although often it is. I've felt it praying, and I've felt it watching puppies play. It's been there when I gazed at a mountain range, heard a lovely symphony passage, felt the closeness of holding my Dad's hand when he was old and sick, watched a child learn to trust her own abilities, studied a masterful painting, or listened to a friend offer understanding and comfort. In each of these experiences I was caught up, taken outside of myself and my daily concerns, and set right. Joy has come in good times and in hard times, in the midst of a loving family or group of friends, and it has come to me when I was alone and afraid. The trick is to be ready, be willing to give it its due place, learn from it, and be grateful. It has its reasons, and they are not ours to predict or understand. It's a precious gift, not something we can plug in and turn on whenever we want.

One time soon after my husband Alan died, I was driving to Nevada, where I had agreed to work for a few days. I was sad and frightened about many things. Even so, I couldn't help but notice how beautifully the lowering sun had washed transparent layers of pink and purple over the mountains, and they were crowned with a light frosting of snow. In my loneliness and frustration I spoke out loud, "Oh, Alan, I wish you could see this!" Just then, I heard him say, in the clearest, sweetest voice, "You should see it here!" The rush of joy told me he was fine, in a better place, and I could let go and move forward. I never heard that voice again, and I never needed to.

We are all, every day, standing on holy ground. Most of us never notice. But when we do, oh, when we do take or allow a break in our constant self-involvement, our repeated mental murmurings about wanting and needing and hurting and being angry, tired, and treated unjustly, then, just then, joy has a chance at us. We can be fully alive, then, nailed to the moment, bleeding tears of gratitude, expanding so quickly that it hurts and forces us to inhale sharply. There's a book called Authentic Happiness by Martin Seligman, a past president of The American Psychological Association. In it, he encourages us to savor joy and to fight against habituation—which means, roughly, getting so used to something that we don't think much of it at all. Savoring is like rolling something around in your mouth to get all the possible taste from it. Simply, it means paying attention. So for example, the next time there's a gorgeous sunset, stop what you're doing and look, really look, at it, and say thanks. If you practice studying these mountaintops of joy very closely, they will be easier to recall when you're in a valley of sadness or discouragement. If you remember them well, you can begin to plan a path that takes you back to those mountaintops. I'll be waiting for you there.

Workbook Questions:

1. Write a few words describing three experiences that have brought you joy.
2. Has joy ever surprised you by its sudden arrival? What did you focus on then?
3. What activity takes you outside of your normal self-involvement? Have you ever experienced joy through that activity?
4. What other activities might help open you to experiences of joy?
5. The next time you sense that joy is about to happen for you, what can you do to more fully experience and savor it?

Love

- How to tell if it's "real" love
- The dangers of obsessive love
- How to grow into the satisfying mature form of love

It's said that true love wants what is best for the other person; while romantic love just wants the other person. That about wraps it up, all right. Obviously, there are many kinds of love, for we love our country, our family, chocolate ice cream, the mercy of God, pink shoes of just the right design, the cute kid down the block, the newest baby kitten, poetry that makes us think, music that makes us cry, picnics, fireworks, and way too many things that aren't good for us. Love is our duty and our joy, and it's also our passion and our madness. It brings heat to life, and also the cold eternity of loneliness. It's a marvel and a mystery. I'll tell you what I know of it, and also tell you up front that you're going to have to discover a lot of this for yourself.

Lots of love is like currency, trading with others, making sure we're not getting cheated. This is sometimes mistaken for friendship, and nearly always cheapens the relationship. "I don't have to call her; it's her turn to call". "We did what you wanted to do last weekend, now I want to go to the movies, so we should". Why are we keeping score? What's the prize if we win?

Some love is obligation, pure and simple. "Come here and let Great-aunt Irene give you a kiss." "You know your father is tired after work. You can mow the lawn for him". When there's no joy in the presence of the other, only calculating duty, it's a mild form of obedience indeed. Add the joy, and obligation's love becomes something special, something to be grateful about.

Loyalty and gratitude birth another form of love, patriotism. It's intense at times, especially when under attack, and on the whole, healthy and fulfilling. The danger is that it seems to require thinking less of others from other places, and I can't find those instructions anywhere in my manual for living.

Romantic love gets all the press. Most popular music, most best-selling novels, most magazine covers, most gossip, all serve up the latest examples and ideas about romance. You'd think after all these centuries we wouldn't need to have it explained to us over and over, but it appears to be new for every single person, and the learning has to start at the beginning again. So, in case you're about to experience this, I can tell you that it's a temporary form of insanity. This love causes you to see everything you want in another person, and to desire to be with that person more than you desire to eat or sleep. You become blind to the charms of others, and deaf to the pleas of your friends for some of your attention. You believe everyone else is blind, too, and won't notice or mind your public displays of affection. You believe your parents have turned into tyrants, conspiring to keep you from enjoying your love on a full-time basis. This insanity has a purpose, which is to establish families and homes, but in a culture like ours, where education takes so many years, the timing is usually pretty far off. Nevertheless, for all its madness and insularity, romantic love is a mountaintop of life, and lucky indeed is the person whose love is returned.

In a good marriage, the kind I hope you'll both have, romantic love is always there, but mellower and more sane as the years go by, with contentment, companionship, and mutual care growing more visible than the passions. When you see older people walking hand in hand, that's what we're all aiming for. As Antoine de Saint-Exupery so beautifully put it, "Life has taught us that love does not consist in gazing at each other but in looking outward together in the same direction." A lifetime of such deep sharing is a blessing and a gift.

The selfless kind of love found in these good marriages is also present in agape, a kind and giving love directed towards others. This is what makes it possible to love people whom you do not particularly like. You may even dislike them, but nevertheless you want the best for them, and growth, and grace. And once this love develops in the soul, it spreads in all directions, helping, lifting up, caring for, giving to and sharing with others just because the love is there and it has its urgencies. It's a gift from heaven, and allows us to reach the highest levels of humanity, those paths trod by Mother Teresa, Mahatma Gandhi, Martin Luther King, and all the saints. This outpouring love fuels compassion, charity, and sacrifice, and is one of the most noble forms of love, much to be sought.

When people talk of love, they rarely mention self-love, except as an embarrassing aside, referring to vanity or excess pride. Bur self-love is an essential component of all the other forms. You just can't pour out of an empty bucket; there must be a solid self there to do the giving. We must love, accept, and forgive ourselves first before we can begin to love, accept, and forgive others. The model is there, of course, in the Scriptures. The ode to love in I Corinthians 13 is among the most beautiful descriptions ever penned. Besides being inspirational, true, and soaring poetry, it's a wonderful litmus test. Read it over when you think you love someone; it will tell you the truth.

Workbook Questions

1. Have you ever tried to love your enemies? How did it go?
2. Can you truly say you want what is best for someone you love, even if that doesn't meet your expectations?
3. What could you do to add the joy of love to an obligation you feel toward someone?
4. Does the expression of love for yourself make you uncomfortable? How can you move toward more acceptance and regard for yourself?

Forgiveness

- What to do about that old grudge you're still carrying
- How to stop feeling like a victim
- How to stop feeling guilty and learn to forgive yourself

Forgiveness is one of the highest forms of human goodness, and one of the hardest to practice, of course. It is so difficult that we have to take refuge in wit. Hillary Rodham Clinton has remarked that "In the Bible it says they asked Jesus how many times you should forgive, and he said 70 times 7. Well, I want you all to know that I'm keeping a chart." I love that, because of course she knows that 70 times 7 just means as often as you have to, and she also knows how hard it is, so she's pretending that she can quit forgiving after that number of times. I'll bet her husband alone can be the occasion for much more than that!

When I was in junior high, my friend's cousin came into town one Spring vacation. He was a high school boy, very good looking, and we spent a lot of time together. He asked me if I could go to his prom, and I was so excited—a high school prom! Later on, I found out it was all a joke, he had already planned to go with a girl from his school, and was just playing with my feelings. I was led on, lied to, and let down—hard. I was so hurt, that I sent him a note that said "Time heals all wounds; I only hope it wounds all heels!" It took me years to get over that (the hurt, not the note; I kind of liked that), and in all that time I never really trusted any of the guys. Lack of forgiveness probably cost me a lot of happiness during that time.

But it takes a lot of work and a lot of strength to forgive, it's not for sissies or weaklings. Mahatma Gandhi, that hero of India's independence, was an expert on that. He said "The weak can never forgive. Forgiveness is an attribute of the strong." Just in case you have any doubt about that, I'd like you to think of someone you know who carries a grudge, someone who, the first thing they do in the morning is put that chip on their shoulder. "I'm the one who hates!" They sound tough, they look tough, but Gandhi would have us understand that they are truly weak. They need that hatred to feel like somebody, because that's all they've got. How sad.

Carrying hate around, like a chip on the shoulder, gradually destroys your humanity. There's no doubt that many, many people would be justified in feeling hatred towards others who have harmed them, but that's not the point. Righteous indignation, righteous anger, is only useful so far as it gives you energy to solve the problem and prevent it from happening again. When its only purpose is revenge, it becomes twisted, and so, eventually, do you. Gandhi talked about the futility of revenge in this way: "If we practice an eye for an eye and a tooth for a tooth, soon the whole world will be blind and toothless". There are nations that have hated each other for generations. People kill each other to avenge the prior murder of their cousin, or brother, or neighbor, and then they are killed to avenge that killing, and the senseless compulsion of hate destroys any hope of peace, of love, of contentment, of normal life for them, their children, and their children's children forever.

But there is a different way, a difficult way of forgiveness and grace. In South Africa, where history could easily produce revenge killings for decades, the people have instead established reconciliation tribunals, where they come together to acknowledge past evil and to forgive, and to learn to live together in spite of the harm once done. I am in absolute awe of their grace and power. Bishop Desmond Tutu, one of the leaders in this process, has affirmed his belief that forgiveness is part of real politics. It, he says, "doesn't mean condoning what has been done. It means taking what happened seriously . . . drawing out the sting in the memory that threatens our entire existence." Without such forgiveness, the future would be bleak, a condemnation to continue the hatred and bitterness.

So we see from these heroes that forgiveness provides a path for healing between people, even people who have harmed one another with terrible cruelty. And we have also heard that forgiveness provides a path for personal healing as well. To stay in an unforgiving state of hatred means to be always a victim, powerless against future hurt, trapped in the memory of past hurt. To forgive means to become the stronger one, to share that strength with the oppressor. I understand now that my friend's cousin was just testing his appeal, just seeing if he could get more than one girl to say she wanted to go to the prom with him. He must have felt pretty insecure. And so I understand, and forgive, and am released from the hurt.

Forgiving others is so difficult, but it's not the hardest thing. That is forgiving oneself. To know that you have wronged another person, to know that you have fallen short, to know your sin, that is far more painful than to know someone else has failed. And yet, we are to forgive this, too, for we have been forgiven. It's arrogance to hold that failing in our mind's eye when God has wiped it from his. If He can forgive, and has forgiven, who are we to withhold that from ourselves? To insist that we cannot forgive is to say that we have higher standards than God, and that is surely foolishness. There are far, far better things to do with our energy and our time than bemoan our failings endlessly. Admit them, confess them, let them go, and get on with the business of life.

Workbook Questions:

1. What can you do to begin to forgive someone who has wronged you? Can you try to understand why they acted as they did?
2. How can you advocate for more forgiveness in your community? Why should you?
3. What secret guilt of your own do you need to examine, understand, and forgive?

Creativity

- Learn the 4 steps to increased creativity
- Try a simple game to measure your current creativity level
- Understand why those who are a little different may hold the key to solutions

Like many other lucky people, I've had a refrigerator door full of grandchildren's drawings and paintings from the time of their earliest enthusiastic doodles. Those drawings and paintings have been wonderful for me to have—indicators of affection and creativity! We usually think of creativity in just that way, as having to do with art, or maybe music, but I'd like to help you think about it in a much broader sense.

Creative people are people who are different, and in their difference, they change the world. They are the tinkerers, who can't leave well enough alone. They are ones who don't accept authority quietly. They may be troublemakers and nuisances, upsetting the balance. They aren't like everybody else, and that's why they are so valuable. I know that for most young people, being like everybody else provides some security, some reassurance that they're going to come through adolescence at least as OK as their friends. But these folks are on to something even more interesting and worthwhile than popularity—they can't seem to help making things a little different. And, often, that difference is a little better. When you think about it, every invention, every change, every improvement was begun by some creative soul just expressing their dissatisfaction with the way things are.

You can get a general idea of your own and other people's creativity by playing a simple game. Name a common object—a paper cup, or a telephone, or almost anything. Then, give everybody one minute to write down all the uses they can think of for that object—from the boring and normal to the wild and unthinkable. At the end of a minute, count how many each person has, and give double, or even triple, points for the really wild ones. This shows you two faces of creativity, the fluidity, of flow, of lots of ideas, and the outrageousness that comes from being able to combine two ideas that don't usually go together.

If you aren't satisfied with your creativity score in that game, or if you just would like more of it, there's a 4-step method to boost creativity I can recommend. It deliberately uses both halves, or hemispheres, of your brain, so you have everything working for you. Step one is to research the problem. Let's say you haven't been doing well at eating breakfast, even though you know it's important. So you research it, to find out just why breakfast is important, and what you should be eating—protein, or starch, or vitamins, or something else. Step two is to stop thinking about it consciously, to assign it to your right brain, to work on. It really helps if you can keep your left brain out of the way during this step. To do that, do something repetitive to keep it busy, like swimming, or playing cards, or practicing piano, so the right brain can incubate, or "cook" the problem. After awhile, the right brain will hand you an answer—it's that "Aha!" sensation, and it's very exciting. That's called illumination, like a light bulb going on, and it is step three. There's a slight problem, though. The right brain isn't in very close touch with reality—it might hand you a solution that's illegal, or physically impossible. So, step four is to get the left brain working again on what is called validation, or checking out the solution for its practicality. So, back to the breakfast problem, you do your research, then tell your right brain to figure out an answer, then do something else, expecting an answer soon—let's say when you wake up the next morning. Well, your creative right brain might tell you to have a driver bring you a breakfast while you walk to school or work. That's not very practical, because your funds this month just don't include enough for the driver's salary. But, there is a good idea hidden there, and step four will help you find it—what could you eat that's healthy and easy, while on your way, so it doesn't take extra time? Maybe fruit, or a breakfast bar, or some other easy to carry food.

I used this method when I wrote a book about Fresno. There were chapters on subjects that were new to me, so I researched them carefully and interviewed lots of experts. Then, for step two, I went to the pool and swam laps, not thinking about the book. When I finished, I changed and went to the computer and the words just seemed to come out of my fingers. But, because I knew my information may have been less than perfect, I looked it over carefully and submitted it to an editor to check again. The four steps helped me to write a book I've been proud of about the town we lived in.

While we've been thinking about creativity, I hope you've also been re-thinking how the different people are treated at school, at work, and in the community. Who knows what genius, what wisdom, might be hidden in that person's future? Somebody, somewhere, in your generation carries the solution to nearly every one of our most difficult and painful world problems. And, that someone is sure to be just a little different. I'd bet a little kindness and respect would help bring those solutions out even sooner.

Workbook Questions:

1. Where in your life have you already expressed your creativity? How did it feel?
2. Are you willing to be considered a bit of a nuisance if you always try to improve things?
3. Name one problem you'd like to solve. Now, apply the 4-step creativity process described here to that problem. Write down the solutions you develop, and keep improving them.

Grace

- Evaluate the physical, emotional, and spiritual aspects of grace
- Discover the rewards of a giving spirit
- Learn how grace affects your ability to listen and understand

When I was in sixth grade or so, my body was growing and changing, every day it seemed. My arms would be longer in the morning than they were the night before; at least that was my excuse for so often spilling the milk at the breakfast table. The one thing I was sure I didn't have was grace.

And, how I coveted it! I suspected, already, as Park Benjamin has said, that "beauty and grace command the world". But I've learned that there are many manifestations of grace, so that we all can aspire to at least some of them, whether or not we ever achieve physical grace. And now I know, with Bo Lazoff, that "We're all stumbling toward the light with varying degrees of grace at any given moment".

If you take simple good manners and multiply the source and effect many times over, you get the kind of consideration sometimes called grace. It doesn't notice that your face is dirty or your clothes don't quite cover you, it doesn't show any pain or difficulty or hesitation or inconsistency of its own, it yields minor points quickly so as not to stumble unnecessarily on the path to agreement, and it reflects in outward life the inner harmony of the person. To be listened to by someone with this kind of grace is to feel deeply heard and cherished. James Thurber describes the experience this way: "Those rare souls whose spirit gets magically into the hearts of men leave behind them something real and warmly personal . . . the grace of a fine spirit pervades the places through which it has passed".

So it's not so much that I, or we, need ballet lessons to acquire grace, but that we pay some attention to acquiring a grace of the spirit while we struggle to gain more grace in our bodies. There's a wonderful book, *Ordinary Grace,* that considers how it is that some individuals become extraordinarily helpful, understanding, and compassionate towards others. The people the psychologist author interviews are from every income and educational level, but all share the willingness to give, whether a sandwich or a kidney, and all testify that they receive as much or more than they give. The Buddhists call this *tonglen,* mutual giving and receiving. It's the connectedness we have when we open ourselves to grace. It's the way we were meant to relate to each other, all the time.

Aunt Heather worked a couple of summers at an Easter Seals camp, giving very sick kids a chance to do the silly, wonderful things that kids always do at camp. She came away from that experience beautifully grounded, well connected with others who had been there, and more sure than ever of her calling. You probably remember packing Christmas gift bags for kids in La Cruz last year, and all the fun things that were donated by so many caring people. Because you spent that afternoon helping, more than 200 children got something to make their holiday special, and you got something, too, in your growth in responsibility, understanding, and caring, and, yes, grace.

There's a young black Rottweiler down the street whose owner is careless at best. She's chained closely, isn't fed regularly, and sometimes the water bucket is tipped over for days on end. I've been taking her food and water every day. She's just a pup, and very loving and appreciative, and I've been worrying about her future. I mentioned it to a new friend of ours at dinner the other night. Turns out he'd just had a burglary and another attempted one, and was more than ready for a dog that looked fierce. Well, the pup's owner got greedy and set an incredibly high price for a dog that has no special papers, or even the basic shots. I waited several days to see if the transaction had taken place anyway, losing hope as the days went by. Finally, I got up the nerve to call our new friend, and he laughed and said the high price was no problem, since a robbery would cost much more, and he'd instruct someone to go buy the dog for him right away. My relief is immense, since we're leaving for a few weeks and the dog wouldn't be cared for otherwise. Such a small thing in the universe, but that's the way many manifestations of grace come to us, with unexpected ease, with immediate relief, even with laughter. The grace of that friend healed my hurt and anxiety. Henry Ward Beecher says that's the way it works, "God appoints our graces to be nurses to other men's weaknesses."

Those with the gift of grace see themselves in the place of the other, and with all humility, give what they would like to receive if that were true. It's common to hear them say, "There, but for the grace of God, go I", and to understand the suffering and need of the other as their own. This ability to see the other as like us, or even as ourselves, is central to the Hasidic story of Heaven and Hell. It seems that a visitor saw a long table loaded with delicious foods and hungry people sitting all around it, each armed with a three-foot spoon. The people sitting at the banquet couldn't figure out how to get the food into their mouths, and so they were starving in the midst of plenty. The visitor was then taken to an identical room with a long, bountiful table and happy, rejoicing people, who also each had in their hands three-foot long spoons. The difference, the distinction that made this room a place of joy was that, here, they had learned to feed each other. And so it is that grace feeds the giver and the one given to, and both thrive.

Workbook Questions:

1. Who, in your life experience, has been a really good listener to you? Is this a form of grace you'd like to develop?
2. Do you believe that the giver also receives? Can you think of an example from your life?
3. Consciously look for people who express the considerate gift called grace in this letter. Would you like to be more like them? How could you begin?

Hope

- How to encourage hope in the midst of despair
- Learn to make peace with loss, and to become open to the new
- Understand the natural rhythm of grief and recognize the moment of transition into new growth

When my husband Alan died on our honeymoon in Mexico, your father came to retrieve my shattered self. I'd been so blissfully happy that I owned nothing black and had to go buy a dress. I remember trying to be a polite hostess through the funeral, trying to see to the guests, trying to fend off the panic that threatened to overwhelm me. And then it stopped threatening and just did it. The next year was one long, bleak, angry howl of pain at the injustice of his death, the cruelty of his family's hostile and accusing reaction, the hopelessness of having lost our future. There were over one thousand hang-up calls to be certain what was left of my sanity never had a moment's peace. In the haunting and the torment, the discouragement and the despair, I kept working, kept praying, kept taking care of what I could, not because I wanted to, but because I knew I had to. Very gradually, a little calm crept into my soul, and as I helped others in my training seminars to deal with their conflict and change, a bit of the teaching reflected its light back on me, and hope began to build a small nest in my heart.

The most lyrical and lovely celebration of hope I know is found in Emily Dickenson's poetry:

> Hope is the thing with feathers
> That perches in the soul
> And sings the tune without the words
> And never stops—at all . . .
>
> No.254, St.1, 1861

But it does stop. There are times when darkness is all around us, when pain is too hard to bear, when the future fails to beckon, when no one seems to care. What I have for you in this letter is like starter for sourdough bread. It's the little bit I know about how, when sadness reigns in your heart, to encourage hope's return. It's what I know about how to retrieve hope when it's utterly gone, how to welcome its nest-making and ask it to live in your heart once again.

First, what not to do. Don't brush off the pain; don't listen to people who tell you not to sweat the small stuff, and that it's all small stuff. They lie—it is not all small stuff! Fear, pain, terror, sadness, and loss are all too horribly real, and they can and do knock the insides—the joy, the dreams, the abilities—right out of us. The Jews have a tradition of sitting Shivah for seven days after a family member's death, acknowledging the reality of the loss, absorbing the pain, letting it have its way and mourning what will never be again. It's a healthy tradition, far better than burying the hurt under pretty words and false optimism. Once the pain has had its day, it pulls away, and we can make our peace with what we have lost and begin to look toward the future once again. We can't see the future, of course, so the view is murky, but we begin moving toward it anyway. Ready or not, here I come! And it's not something or someone out there who may be ready or not, but me, tentatively, fearfully trying to live again.

Soon enough in our shaky new start, we hit a bump and fall on our face. We wait and wail a little, and look around for rescue. But no one is there to help, so we have to nurse our own wounds, and find the strength to get up and try moving forward again. The next time we hit a bump we get discouraged. Won't the pain ever stop? Maybe the third or fourth time we fall, as we're lying there feeling sorry for ourselves, we notice that this time, when we fell, we were a little further along the path, a little higher up, than the last time. When we notice that, something incredible happens—we see that we are beginning to make progress, and hope kicks in, lightening our load and impelling us further and faster toward the future.

As far as I can tell, hope only comes to us while we're already moving forward. It isn't there to start the movement, it arrives as we move, and it brings energy, vision, optimism, and a host of other gifts. We have to trust that those gifts will come, and move on our own without them at first, even though it's the last thing we want to do, and we weep the whole time. I think we have to prepare for this by very deliberately saying goodbye to whatever we've lost, and just as deliberately turning our thoughts and behaviors toward that unseen, unknowable future. It takes courage, and stamina, and trust to go on, but going on is the only thing to do, believing that hope will soon take you by the hand. You get some evidence that you're doing this right, because once hope kicks in, the path gets a little smoother, things become a little easier, movement a little quicker. You can smile again, give again, and love again, and feel the feathers in your soul tickle just a little.

The cruelest thing dictators do is rob the people of hope. The most unkind thing a parent can do to their child is to pretend to see their future failure: "You'll never be any good!" We have to believe there's something better coming, even though today's evidence for that is sparse. Hope feeds us, sustains us, supports us, and transforms us. It's a conversation between me and my God. If I only will find the courage to try, He will take my hand to lead and encourage me, using the gift of hope. Every Spring, every sunrise, every rainbow, reminds us that hope is real. May it sustain you all your lives.

Workbook Questions:

1. Have you ever lost hope? If so, what was the most helpful thing for you at that point? What might you do differently next time?
2. Why is it important to fully experience grief and loss before moving forward?
3. Has there been someone whom you have discouraged? Can you help to restore hope to that person?

Faith

- What builds and sustains faith?
- Who and what you put your faith in deeply affect you
- Faith alone is insufficient

Since I'm writing to you about the important things in life, this one just has to be included, even though it's extremely private and very tough to nail down into sound bites. Let's start with the best description of all, in Hebrews 11:1, "Now faith is the substance of things hoped for, the evidence of things not seen". The chapter goes on to give a glorious history of women and men who stepped into the unknown trembling, to obey and act on faith. By so doing, their deeds changed lives, changed history, and set standards of courage and reverence for us all.

The words, "substance" and "evidence" from Hebrews clarify the difference between hope and faith. Hope has an element of uncertainly, of wishfulness, but faith is certain. You have faith, for instance, in your parents' love, because of the evidence of years of unwavering devotion, and the substance of meals and clothes and other needed things freely given. You probably have faith in the love of others in your life, faith in the love of God, and in the law, and in education, and perhaps a few other things.

Talking about, and confessing to, faith is natural for those of us with a strong church background, because we work at making faith in God a part of our everyday lives. But in the world at large it just isn't fashionable. I've often wondered why people who are very intelligent in most respects have this huge hole in their understanding. It's as if they don't want to face the really big issues of life, where laboratory evidence and experimental results fail to offer much guidance. Maybe they'll come around eventually, as they realize that the most meaningful aspects of life are not particularly measureable. As the old saying has it, nobody ever says on their deathbed, "Gosh, I wish I'd spent more time at the office!". The really important parts of life, like joy, and hope, and love, and, yes, faith, are known by all who will look at the intangible along with the rational. Even though it's difficult to understand, there are some facts and attributes about faith that we can and do know.

There's a leadership parable attributed to a French poet that fills in some of the facts about faith. It goes like this:

> He said, "Come to the edge",
> They said, "No, we will fall,"
> He said, "Come to the edge",
> They said, "No, no, we will surely fall."
> He said again, "Come to the edge", and they did.
> And, he pushed them.
> And, they flew.

Their stepping to the edge despite their fears took faith, faith in their leader. His insistence that they come took faith, faith that they were ready to soar. It's a frightening, breathtaking, totally heart stopping scenario, and that's what faith is like in the crunch, which is when we're likely to notice it, and to need it. Because they both had faith, and their faiths intermingled, something extraordinary happened. So, one fact about faith is that it's interactive. Whatever you have faith in, whatever you bring your faith to, deeply affects you.

Faith is also solid and dependable. I surprised one of my counseling clients, a father worried that his kids didn't understand or appreciate his love for them, by telling him that he's like the floor. It's there, so reliable, so unremarkably at our service, that we never think to doubt it. We never step carefully, we just trust the floor to be there, and we never say "Thank you", either. Like a good father, faith is the flooring for our lives, protecting us from the dirty stuff and holding the rest of our dwelling securely in place, day after day, without even being noticed.

Faith is also honest. There are no traps, no tricks, in faith. No crafty thoughts, no sidelong glances, no dancing around the edges of the truth, no cunning angling for the best interpretation. It's plain, and you don't need a university degree to have it. Many writers and thinkers have noticed that the people who lead the simplest lifestyles have the most apparent faith. Maybe all that stuff the rest of us have and do really gets in the way.

Although you can't hold faith in the palm of your hand, it can hold you in the palm of its hand. And it does, in the worst of times, to give strength, courage, endurance, and the ability to do terrible and fearsome things. Abraham was ready to sacrifice his beloved son, Isaac, by faith, and he and his wife, when they were of an age to just sit back and put their feet up, founded a nation by faith. When you reflect on a time in your life where you don't remember how you got through it, faith was there, carrying you and keeping you safe.

As wonderful as faith is, it is not enough. We're taught that, "And now abideth faith, hope, charity, these three; but the greatest of these is charity" (I Cor.13:13). We're also taught that "Faith without works is dead" (James 2:20). So, while life has no purpose and no future without faith, we must add to it in our character both a spirit of charity and a practice of doing good.

Even here, faith can help. In order to build a habit of doing good, we have to have faith that it is worthwhile, in spite of the enormity of the needs in the world and our individual inability to meet them all. In order to develop a spirit of charity towards others, we have to have faith that our loving thoughts and actions will bring out their best, as well. These are not simple matters, but a discipline of living that, in order to be sustained even when there is no visible reward, requires a calm certainty, and the name for that certainty is faith.

Workbook Questions:

1. Name four people or things in which you have great faith. Why? On what evidence did you develop this faith?
2. Has your own faith helped shape your history? Will it shape your future?
3. Has your faith ever "held you in the palm of its hand?" How did you grow as a result?

Gratitude

- Why expressing gratitude is good for you—mentally, physically, spiritually
- How grateful expressions can help heal relationships
- Why it's important to voice your appreciation to others now

Over the years, I've gotten many very sweet thank-you notes from you both, demonstrating that you already know something about gratitude, and how to express it. Those notes may have been a bit of a chore, but there's much more to understanding how important thankfulness is. For starters, what are you most grateful about right now? Something small, something huge, something unexpected? What are you going to do with those grateful feelings? I hope your answer is that you're going to let them out, and spread them around. In the words of that old hymn, "Count your many blessings, and you will be singing as the days go by". And one of the newer praise songs instructs us to "Give thanks with a joyful heart". What it doesn't tell us, but it's true anyway, is that giving thanks is one way to get a joyful heart.

There are some unhappy people who can't think of anything they're grateful for. They treat everything that's done for them as their due, and expect that everyone is giving them as little as possible. After awhile, they're probably right about that second part, because no one wants to be around such a sourpuss. How much more fun it is to give something to someone you know will be ecstatic about it, and tell you so!

Gratitude only starts as a duty that your mom and dad told you to take care of. It grows into having an open mind and an open heart, and noticing the bountiful blessings all around you each and every day. It's terrifically good for you to do that. In a survey recently conducted by spirituality.com, over eighty percent of the people who responded said that gratitude relieved depression, reduced stress, built better physical health, and strengthened positive attitudes. Many researchers have found that the active practice of gratitude reduces both tension and anger.

So how do you develop that attitude of gratitude? What does an active practice of gratitude mean in real life? The Jewish teachings of the *Kabellah* instruct the learner to find 100 things each day to be grateful for. Others have found that devoting 10 or 15 minutes daily to prayerful appreciation for goodness in their lives, both great and small, helps to develop the spirit of gratitude. Some families practice the attitude in family time discussion, giving each person a chance to mention several things they are grateful for. Dr. Martin Seligman, in *Authentic Happiness*, urges the active practice of gratitude with other people. By telling someone what, exactly, you are grateful for in your relationship with them, you not only build their confidence and joy, but you strengthen your own positive mental health as well.

Many, many times I found gratitude to be the key to healing relationships, and to finding a way to work together better in the future. Often I'd have a small business group with a history of conflict off on a retreat somewhere, trying to create a better working atmosphere with them. Sometimes we'd get stuck, and so I would trot out a gratitude exercise that never failed. We'd sit around a table, say, 15 of us, and I'd ask each person to number a page from one to fifteen. Then, starting with the person to my right, each would be assigned a number. Everyone there had to, next to the corresponding number on their page, write one sentence telling what it was about that person that they appreciated. Now, remember that these people disliked each other enough that someone had paid good money to bring me in to help them fix things! So some of them had to work pretty hard to think of something they appreciated, but eventually, everyone did. No one could skip a line, all had to be filled in.

Then, one at a time, each person would stand and everyone had to read the sentence they had written about that person. All the statements were positive, although some were pretty faint praise. Nevertheless, there were tears and smiles, and cries of joy, "I didn't know you felt like that!" Next, when all had spoken, each person tore off the strip of paper with their sentence on it and gave it to the person it was about. I had supplied everyone with a heavy sheet of colored paper and a glue stick, and they all made a poster to hang near their desk with their co-workers comments of appreciation on it. So, each had clear, unarguable evidence of the appreciation their co-workers felt toward them, to inspire and uplift them when the going got rough again. Sometimes I'd visit their office again years later and those posters would still be there; that's how much they meant.

How sad that we don't always make the time to tell others how we appreciate them. Years after my mom died, I'm still writing the occasional letter to her, saying all the things I wish I'd said when there was time. When Alan had his heart attack, I called the doctor from the hotel front desk, and then went back to our room and sat with him holding hands while we waited. We had a few minutes to say how much we loved and appreciated each other, and then he was gone. If I hadn't told him, and heard him tell me, those things, how much harder that next year alone would have been.

So today would be a good day, before you forget or lose the chance, to tell someone how much you appreciate them. Today would be a good day to mention to God a few of the things that you're grateful for. Today would be a good day to remind yourself that you have this good day, and isn't it a beautiful gift? Living your life with a heart full of gratitude is the best thank-you card of all.

Workbook Questions:

1. List 15 things you are grateful for, right now. Have you thanked the source of these things?
2. Think of a troubled or strained relationship in your life. Despite that, is there something about the other person that you can appreciate? Can you tell them that?
3. Have you developed an attitude that the world "owes" you? How can you change that to be more grateful and less bitter? What will you gain from that change?

Wisdom

- What wisdom looks and feels like in practice
- How wisdom differs from knowledge
- Ancient, powerful process for attaining wisdom

The fear of the Lord is the beginning of wisdom, according to the 1662 Prayer Book of the Church of England. That's a good place to start, for one sure indicator of wisdom is humility. Wisdom is a very different thing from knowledge, which so often carries with it pridefulness. There are other differences, too. By necessity, knowledge has to do with the past, but wisdom points toward the future, toward a worthwhile way of living. Knowledge accumulates fact after fact; wisdom discards all nonessentials, eliminating everything but the simple, powerful truth at the core of something. Immanuel Kant contrasted the two this way; science is organized knowledge; wisdom is organized life. And finally, knowledge looks outward, to the thoughts of others. Wisdom looks within, to the meditations of one's own soul.

Confucius taught that there were three ways to learn wisdom. The easiest is imitation, perhaps of a mentor, but that process may not teach understanding. The hardest is through experience, which may be painful and bitter. Lessons learned in that manner are long-lasting, but very hard-won. It is far more common to come to wisdom through failure than through success. I call this the face-down-in-the-mud method. We don't like that position, so we're ready to learn how not to be there again. The third method Confucius taught is that of reflection, again, the looking within contemplatively.

Ibn Gabirol, in the eleventh century, recommended a five-step process to attain wisdom. The first step is silence. Again, the looking within. The second step is listening, and here the opportunity to learn from others appears again. However, other teachers disagree, saying it's not possible to obtain wisdom from anyone else, but rather it must be discovered by each seeker alone. Step three is remembering, which is far more difficult than it appears. Our memories often get distorted by our fears, our prejudices, our hopes, our dreams, and the remembering of exactly what we learned is threatened by the memory of what we wish we had learned. Step four is practicing the new wisdom, applying it to everyday life and testing its utility and accuracy. And finally, teaching the wisdom to others. As any teacher will tell you, the material is much better organized, remembered, and understood when it is shared with others, even if those others may have to take it only as a starting point for their own journey.

As I've been thinking about wisdom, and how to encourage you to search for it on your own, I thought of some of the characteristics of a wise person. For me, that motivates the search, because I want to be like that. Perhaps it will do the same for you. First, a wise person is calm, well grounded, not easily rattled or angered. The search for wisdom requires a long, patient effort of self-control, which yields calmness as a valuable byproduct. Patience is another benefit of this self-control developed in the search for wisdom. Patience helps the individual to be tolerant of others, to endure setbacks with grace, to have faith in the long term benefit of the search, and to be superior to the day to day changes in circumstances. The wise person is comfortable with questions and doubt, for that is how they started on the path. A wise person also appreciates the benefits of tempering, of the stress that creates strength. Perhaps because he noticed that these characteristics breed a simplicity and grace of spirit, Sophocles believed wisdom to be the supreme part of happiness.

Finally, the wise person accepts and celebrates paradox; the truth held in two opposite truths. You know how that works. There's a proverb: He who hesitates is lost. There's also an opposite proverb: Look before you leap. Both are true and wise advice, but they are opposites. Or another: Fools think alike, and its opposite, Great minds run in the same channels. So the ability to tolerate paradox is a characteristic of the wise, to understand that in certain circumstances, two opposites can be equally true. There's some research in the field of psychology into this ability to tolerate paradox, and a related ability, to tolerate ambiguity, multiple possibilities, rather than insisting on simple yes-no answers to problems. It turns out that these abilities are a benefit of higher education which lasts well after the specific ideas and facts learned have faded from memory. Without this ability, whether it's learned in college or self-taught, the individual is destined to an argumentative future, insisting on right or wrong, one way or the other. With this ability, the individual can contemplate complexity in peaceful awareness.

Now, with that peaceful spirit in mind, think of the kinds of people you know or have heard of that pretend to have wisdom. You know, the ones with all the answers to everything. A different picture, isn't it? So, we'll have to add the characteristic of humility in again, for the truly wise person does not call attention to himself or herself, but the prideful person, who really knows much less, does. Interesting, isn't it? One of the comedians my parents used to listen to, George Burns, said it this way: too bad that all the people who really know how to run the country are busy driving taxi cabs and cutting hair. He's referring to the fact that some people in jobs that allow them to talk all day long, do, even without much to say. They haven't caught on to the fact that silence looks like wisdom, even when it's not.

So, where to begin in this journey? Start with a calm, quiet five or ten minutes at the end of each day to contemplate what you have experienced, sift through it for any learning, and make peace with any failings of your own that day. Forgive others, too, for you don't need the weight of any grudges to slow you down. Question quietly any explanations you are given, and see if they are consistent with your experience. Consider other explanations that occur to you, and if you can't decide among them, hold them all in your mind gently while you continue to gather information.

I know it seems very inward, but this will keep your mind open to possibilities. Test your conclusions, and be willing to change them. Always look for the simplest explanation that covers the most events, and you can be confident that you're on the right path. Finally, keep your search for your life's purpose in mind, for as Steven Covey has said, whatever is at the center of our life will be the source of our security, guidance, wisdom, and power. I'd suggest starting with the fear, and the love, of the Lord.

Workbook Questions:

1. How did you make the wisest decision you ever made?
2. Describe the characteristics of the wisest people you know.
3. Can you accept ambiguity and tolerate "it depends" as an answer at times?

Contentment

- Learn to want what you have, more often, more fully
- Savor the life stage you are in right now
- Avoid the cravings that lead to greed and discontent
- Balance ambition and repose

This morning I woke with Max snuggled against the curve of my waist, and Harley nestled into my shoulder on the other side. Both cats were purring in quiet harmony, and they rearranged themselves without a fuss when I stretched and rolled over. Captain Bob reached down and scratched the ears of his twin Golden Retriever puppies, Lassen and Shasta, and I spoke to Nikki, our old Shepherd mix, to see if she was ready to go outside. We sleep in a zoo, and it's not everyone's cup of tea, but it's gentle, friendly, safe, and loving, and I like it that way.

After breakfast, which includes some banana bread with plantains from our yard stirred in, we'll walk the dogs around the neighborhood, stopping to practice our Spanish by greeting the neighbors. I'll admire the royal poinciana tree now in full bloom, a cloud of red orchids, and we'll try to identify the birds so vigorously defending their territories. Then, to church, where I get to have a field day with the pipe organ key I just found on the little keyboard, making the tiny place resound like an old English Presbyterian church. The afternoon will be spent writing, playing music, and swimming, and Captain Bob just said he'd like a little surf fishing this evening for Father's Day. It's a lovely way of life, and for the most part, I'm quite content with the mix of labor and leisure, interaction and solitary, thoughtful work.

The part of me that isn't content is a part I recognize—a bit of ambition, and a bit of greed. Ambition's a healthy impulse, and greed isn't, so it takes a little doing to sort it all out. The secret to contentment, I'm told, is to want what you have, simply that. But as Marie Ebner von Eschenback pointed out a century ago, "To be content with little is hard, to be content with much, impossible". It seems that the more you have, of things, of opportunities, even of education, the more you want. I've learned I can write, now I want to paint. I enjoyed the visit with my daughter and grandson, now I'm lonely for more of them. I received a surprisingly generous check, it was sucked up by repairs and bills so fast that I'm eager for more to come my way.

There's no end to this way of thinking except unhappiness, because there's no end to craving, if once we yield to greed. No matter how lovely your home, how beautiful your children, how impressive your wages, how large your boat or your diamond, there's always one just down the street who has, and flaunts, more. Greed leads to covetousness, which leads to cutting corners to acquire, which leads to a slippery slope, lined in the finest sable, but ending in the erosion of character. And once that's gone, so is any chance at contentment. Greed simply kills it. If you've every wondered why the poets celebrate the contentment of the poor, this explains it. Once the appetites are whetted, satisfaction is elusive indeed.

Ambition is, as I said, a more healthy impulse. Henry Ward Beecher's comment is very helpful: "We are not to make the ideas of contentment and aspiration quarrel, for God made them fast friends. A man may aspire, and yet be quite content until it is time to raise; and both flying and resting are parts of one contentment." So, the secret is in the timing, and I may yet learn to paint, once the writing is done. Because all of us are multi-talented, we can benefit by learning to focus, turning our attention, ambition, and aspiration to one talent, then the next, then the next, in due season, building a rich and contented life layer by layer.

I think the chances are better of living that rich and contented life if we spend a little time burrowing into each layer, exploring, nurturing, detailing, and savoring it. Sometimes in the most unlikely circumstances real contentment lurks just below the surface. Helen Keller found this to be true. "Everything had its wonder, even darkness and silence, and I learn, whatever state I may be in, therein, to be content."

Let's take the layer you two are in now, adjusting to family changes, learning to fit in at school after years of home schooling, becoming young women, with all the transitions and terrors that brings. It would be easy to hurry past this stage, to long for adulthood, or at least full-fledged teen-hood. Any yet, the curiosity you share now, the innocent take on family, local, and national events, the ability to evaluate people's intentions, are real treasures worthy of study and celebration. If you'll spend a little time capturing your thoughts and feelings, perhaps in a journal, you won't overlook the valuable insights you have, right on the tip of your tongue. And maybe, just maybe, you'll be a bit more contented with being who you are just now, at this age and in this place.

I'll try to do the same. There are days I'm tempted to un-retire, go back to "being somebody" full-time again, to the competitive rush and the fat paychecks and the constant pressure. But it passes, and I know that this, for the moment, is enough, to write and walk and swim and seek, to love and live this way, right here, right now, in precarious and precious contentment.

Workbook Questions:

1. What is the best part of the life stage you are in now? How can you enjoy it more fully?
2. Have you ever experienced intense greed and craving? What led to it? Did it result in happiness? How have you overcome it?
3. Who is the most contented person you know? Could you ask that person to talk about what gives them that deep level of satisfaction?

Chapter 2

Skills That Will Help

Setting Priorities

* Develop a meaningful statement of your life's purpose
* The daily list is the essential first step
* Separate the urgent from the important
* Be mindful of why things get your time, attention, and energy

Your Mom used to startle people when she asked, "What's your function?", and she even wore a t-shirt that said that. She used the question to take people down a notch or two, to remind people that they didn't seem real useful at the moment. Although it made me jump when she said it, I liked the question, because life would go a lot better if we had some idea what our function was. Of course, people who talk about it at all usually talk about purpose, rather than function, but they mean the same sort of thing. What are you here for? Not here in this spot at this moment in time, but here on this earth—what is your purpose? Those who find the answer to that question and do it leave a wonderful legacy; those who don't, don't.

You've heard it said from the pulpit and from your friends and relatives, that God has a plan for your life. If we were born with these instructions clearly printed on our palms, we'd have an easier time figuring it all out. Since we're not, it's worthwhile to spend some time once in awhile developing a simple purpose statement to help us keep on track. It's a lot like a company's Mission Statement, which tells the world what they're there for, and why they are better at it and more excited about it than anyone else. To write a purpose statement for now, just decide what excites and interests you and what makes you especially qualified to do that. You'll adjust and maybe totally change that statement from time to time, and that's fine—it's called growth, and it's good. Now, look at that statement frequently—it's a tuning fork, a magnetic north, something that keeps you headed in the right direction. All your activities should support that purpose, and the most important activities—your priorities—are those that are closest to the purpose, and help make it come true.

Since we're all doing something all the time during our whole lives, it might as well be something that advances, or serves, our purpose, don't you think? But, you say, and I can almost hear you, there's all this other stuff to do, and by the time we're done with that, we're too tired to sit around and figure out our purpose in life. OK, fair enough, so let's talk about the process of managing all the things we have to do so that there is time for the important things. There's even a word for that—prioritizing, or setting priorities. Setting priorities takes a small amount of time, and a large amount of concentration, but once it's done, everything else proceeds smoothly.

If you want to use the most popular shortcut in this process, it's an easy, low-tech one. Make a list. That's right, just make a list of what you have to do this day, another list of what you have to do this week, another for this month, and another for this year. I always do the yearly one on New Year's Day, just because there's usually some quiet time then to think about it. Keep the daily one in front of you, and check in on the others every so often. On the daily one, divide things up into three categories, the really important, the medium-level stuff that just has to get done, but isn't very exciting or challenging, and the low-level stuff that wouldn't cause a major problem if you had to skip them today. You can color-code them, or number them 1,2, and 3, or label them A, B, and C; it really doesn't matter, as long as you can tell which are the important ones. Then, it's your job to pay attention to the A level ones every day; the B level ones will get done, because you can't avoid them (like making meals, doing homework, filling up the car gas tank) without having big problems. The C ones will only get done if you have a few minutes of spare time between more important things, and that's fine. You don't have to worry about doing those perfectly, or at all, if there's a real time crunch. Your job is to pay attention to the A ones.

How can you be certain that something is an A level priority? Well, it fits your purpose, it pulls you toward the future, it stretches you and makes you grow, and it takes advantage of opportunity; in other words, it matters more than the other stuff. And, oddly enough, these are the things that are frequently neglected, because they don't have alarms going off, and they're often long-term things that are easy to postpone. It takes real discipline to focus on them, but the payoff is a more meaningful life.

There are some suggestions from the field of time management that help you make real progress on those A level items, even if you can only give them a little time each day. When you're working on one of these, get to a good stopping point before you quit. It often takes some thought to make headway on an A level, and if you just break off the work part way through an idea, it's hard to come up with that thinking again. Include personal time for yourself and for your family in the A level list, so your life stays well-balanced. Whenever you can, make progress on the

A level stuff during your most alert time of the day. The B and C things don't need your best shot, but the A level things do.

Setting priorities is a sensible and rewarding way to make sure that you're the one deciding what the result of each day's living is. You determine what gets your time, attention and energy, and that's a responsible way to live. That's the day by day, step by step way to build your legacy, to live "on purpose" Not paying attention to priorities is like living "by accident", in the default mode, not good enough for anyone as bright and caring as you! My purpose right now, and for the last twenty years, is to tell the truth as I understand it. I hope this piece of the truth helps you find your own purpose and fulfill it.

Workbook Questions:

1. Name the two most important things you need to get done today. How do these two things serve your purpose?
2. Can you find ways to trade, barter, delegate, give away, or ignore your lowest-level tasks at least two days a week? Then, use that time for your top priorities.
3. Write a brief statement of purpose for yourself. What are you here (on earth) for? What excites you about that?

Taking Smart Risks

- Use a simple analytical tool to help overcome the fear of risk
- Real rewards are usually associated with real risks
- Learn to tell the difference between smart risks and foolish ones

If you're athletic, or outspoken, you've already shown courage, and that's great! Courage helps you take risks, and that usually leads to excitement, a feeling of living fully, and the rewards of leadership. However, if it's undisciplined, courage may cause you to take foolish risks, far more likely to lead to harm than to rewards. So the trick is to learn to take risks, but only, or at least mostly, smart risks.

Let's say it's a hot day and you're having a picnic by a riverbank, somewhere new to you. It's very tempting to run from the bank and dive in, isn't it? But what if there's a log just under the water, out of sight? You wouldn't want to hit your head on it, so it's better, not to stay out of the water, but to check it out well before jumping in. That's a smart risk, and the reward is feeling cooler safely.

Not too long ago, our government abandoned its color-coded terrorist warning system—orange for one level of danger, red for another, and so on. I'm not sure exactly why that system worked so badly, but I think it was because most people think the government's information sometimes isn't very good, and the danger is usually so local that warning everybody, say, to avoid all airports, just doesn't make sense, and it inconveniences a lot of people. But wouldn't it be great if we could have a color coded danger warning sign attached to the risks we want to take? Almost never take a red one. Once in awhile, go for an orange one, just dive in on a yellow one, and so forth. It doesn't work that way, of course, but I found a system that's almost as good. It's a mathematical formula, and here's how it works.

Imagine that you want to take a road trip, just the two of you, the whole length of California. Lots of people have done that, so you know it can de done, but as new drivers, it's a bit risky for you two. So, I suggest you first ask, "What could possibly go wrong?", and list the answers. For this example, you might have a list that reads, "We'll run out of gas and be far from a station", and "Something will go wrong with the car that we don't know how to fix", and "We'll get lost", and so on. Now that you have a list, ask yourselves two questions, and rate the answers on a scale of 1-5, from low to high. The first question is "How likely is that?". For "We'll get lost", it might be a 2, but for running out of gas, it might be a 4, since you're not used to watching the gauge. Do that for each one, then ask yourselves the second question, "How terrible would it be if that happened?". For "We'll get lost", it might be a 5, and for running out of gas, it might be a 5 as well. Now you have a list of everything that might go wrong, with two numbers after each thing, one for likelihood, and one for level of calamity. Multiply those two numbers for each thing that might go wrong, and you'll have a list of rated disasters. Some things might have really low numbers, and you might decide you can easily tolerate those problems, and don't have to worry about them at all. Others might have high numbers—real dangers. For those, make a plan, it's called a contingency plan, for what you would do if that happened. For example, you might take a cell phone, or a laptop, or rent a car with a GPS system to guide you, to protect yourselves from getting too lost. You might carry extra gas, or make a pact to never let the tank get below ½ full on your trip, so you're always sure of reaching another gas station. That's a simple example, and probably not too scary, but the same technique works to help you decide how to take smart risks that are much more unusual and challenging, and potentially much more rewarding.

The point is not to avoid risk—not at all—because that really is how you find high rewards, both in the stock market and in life. Rather, the point is to analyze risks, take them apart, and evaluate the best way to handle them. Taking smart risks sets you apart from the crowd, it puts you on a playing field populated only by sages and fools. The fools arrived there by accident, and survive by chance, but the sages are there on purpose, and take the test of risk as an entrance exam to a higher level of living. Like kites, we only rise against the wind, and calculated risks are a very brisk breeze indeed, helping us rise quickly and brilliantly.

I've been badly bruised, but not killed, by miscalculated risks. And I've been stunned by the joy of accomplishment in meeting and conquering risks taken with more care and thought. I hope this simple system will help you avoid more of the bruises and find more of the joy.

Workbook Questions:

1. Have you ever taken a risk that now seems foolish? What did you learn in the process?
2. Do you agree that the playing field of risk is populated by fools and sages? Which are you more often like?
3. Using the system described here, analyze the risk for something you've been wanting to do, but have feared.

Setting Goals

- Well-written goals have timelines, action verbs, and personal responsibility
- Learn what motivates you to keep moving towards a goal
- Develop contingency plans to implement when difficulties arise
- Write goals for balance in all the major life arenas

What do you want different in your life next week? Next year? When you're 20, 50, 80? I'll bet you can think of some things you'd like to have different right away, and other things will occur to you as you go along. Very rarely, however, do those things we want to be different in our lives happen by accident, or by themselves. To be most certain that we can steer the direction of our life in a productive and pleasant way, we absolutely must set goals. There's no other way, than to clearly define, make very real in our mind's eye, what we want. There are several tips, tricks, and techniques that make these goals more likely to come true, and I'd like to share some of the best with you.

First, grab a piece of paper and write down a goal—anything you want to have different and better in the future. Then, check the goal for three things. It has to be one you are responsible for; no fair writing goals for other people Next, it has to have a deadline—by when do you want it done? Indefinite, whenever goals just don't happen. Finally, it needs to have a verb in it—you know, an action word, like make, build, increase, decrease, explain, carry. So now, you have a goal statement for you to do with an action verb and a deadline so you can tell what you're supposed to do and by when.

Second, write down all the ways your life is going to be better when you have reached that goal you just wrote. Be specific, and include everything; if it's going to make you happier, say so; if it's going to make people like you better, say so; if it's going to make you smarter about something, say so. These written statements of benefits are the things that you will re-read to keep you going when it gets tough. They are your motivators for this goal.

Now comes the genius part. Write down everything you can think of that might go wrong, and ask other people to help you think of still more things that might go wrong or get in the way. Then, write a simple plan of action for dealing with all those obstacles. Now, you're ready to write down the steps towards your goal. What's today's part of it, tomorrow's part of it, and so on? How will you measure your progress? If it's a goal like losing weight (don't even think of it, Kylie), that's easy, you just get on the scale. If it's a goal like learning French, you'd have to take a test now and then. If it's a goal like running a mile, you start with 100 yards, and then, when you live through that, do more, then still more, and so on.

Now you have a plan of action towards your goal, something to do every day or every week towards it, and a way to measure your progress. You also have lots of good motivators written to keep you moving, and you know what to do if something goes wrong. How could you not succeed? I know this works, because this is how I got the consulting business going, and by using this system, my income increased by five times over my last job as a graduate school dean.

Now you know how to set a goal that's likely to be accomplished, and so the next step is to think about what kinds of goals we should be setting. Let's look at some ways to use this goal setting process to help build a happy, meaningful life that is well-balanced. While many people do some kind of goal setting already, they do it only in certain areas of their lives, and I think they're really missing out on something important. In your personal life (as opposed to work life, when you have a job), many people believe that there are at least six important parts—social life, mental health, financial health, physical health, family life, and spiritual life. I'll bet lots of folks you know can tell you what their financial goals are—to buy a house, to buy a car, to retire someday, to save for a new bicycle, to pay a big bill, or something like that. But probably few people can answer you about their other goals, for family life, mental health, and so on. Not all of the areas are as easy to think about as finance, but you'll get the idea quickly as you go. For example, in mental health, what new thing would you like to learn, and how would you go about it? There's a goal. In social life, what kinds of activities with friends would you like to do that you're not doing now? There's another goal. In spiritual health, are you reading a devotional booklet or Bible chapter daily? If not, there's a goal. In family life, would you like to spend some alone time with a parent once in awhile, just talking? There's a goal. Imagine your life as a delicious pie divided up into six big, luscious pieces. The one you're setting goals for gets to be a wonderful dessert, but the ones you ignore just get old, dried out, and useless. Who would want that kind of pie? Better to pay attention to all the pieces. You see, it's easy, once you start thinking this way.

Because the method I've suggested takes a little time, I don't recommend that you jump into goal setting in all areas of life at once. If you try to pay attention to one or another area each week, by the end of a couple of months, you'll see real progress, and you'll feel much more in control of your life.

Just a couple more words of encouragement. People who set goals are more in charge of their lives, and they get the satisfaction of each success, and the learning from each mistake. People who don't set goals spend their time blaming other people, wishing things were different, and talking about their bad luck. Would you like your life to be based on blaming, wishing, and luck? How about on learning from mistakes and reaping joy and satisfaction from success? I thought so.

Workbook Questions:

1. Write a simple goal describing an improvement in your family life. Evaluate: is this your personal responsibility, does it have a deadline, and is there an action verb in it?
2. Write two things that might go wrong on your way to that goal, and what action you would take to stay on track.
3. Ask a successful person you know whether and how they use goalsetting.

Gaining Persuasiveness

- Develop an ethical foundation for personal influence
- Understand the roles of expertise and fairness in persuasiveness
- Persuasion is power with, not power over, someone

If you ask people what the shortcut to happiness is, I'd bet they'll say getting other people to do what you want them to. Now, I don't believe that's the true path to happiness, but so many people do that books on that topic are popping up all over the place. Of course, it's easy enough to get people to do what you want them to if you're a dictator or a prison guard, but that doesn't count. For most of us, we can't *make* anybody do anything, and it's hard to figure out how to get them to want to do what we'd like. The name for getting someone to do or think what you'd like them to is persuasion. It's your ability to cause the other person to want to change their thoughts and actions. Sometimes it's called influence, and it's well worth working to master the process of honest persuasion.

First of all, there are three foundations for persuasion, and they are not all equally effective. All are somewhat helpful, so don't neglect any of them. The first is logic, getting your argument solidly based on facts. That's good enough to persuade many people, but not all, for nobody pays any attention to facts that don't suit them. Remember, there used to be factual arguments that the earth was flat! So, people can ignore or doubt any facts that don't suit them, and justify it by saying the facts are probably not entirely correct, or will be changed with more information. It pays to know your facts anyway.

The second foundation, empathy, is a little more effective than logic. That means that if you care deeply about something, and it shows, that alone will be persuasive. If you've ever cried or laughed with a character in a book or a movie, you know how strongly you can "feel along" with someone else. The people you are trying to persuade can "feel along" with you, and that may be enough to change their thought or actions.

The third, and most effective, foundation for persuasion is simply your character, what kind of a person they know you to be. Nobody trusts a con artist, but instead, if you are someone known to be honest and reliable, your arguments are pretty darn persuasive just because of your reputation. As Ralph Waldo Emerson said, "What you *are* shouts at me so loudly that I can't hear a word you are saying". Ideally, and most effectively, you'll have all three of these going for you—logic, emotional appeal, and character.

Your personality counts in other ways, too, for effective persuasion. There are several traits or qualities that really make a difference, and even in youth, some of them are already present and can be developed further. The first is sincerity, because nobody is persuaded by a phony. You have to believe in what you're saying. Second is fairness and accuracy. You can't exaggerate and get people to believe you, at least, not more than once. You show fairness also by pointing out what's wrong with your argument, or your position—saying, in spite of that, I still think it's the best thing. Warmth and friendliness count, too—nobody is drawn to the side of someone who's cold and aloof. This is a hard one if you're a little shy, I know, but worth working on. High energy also helps, because it shows your commitment and willingness to work for what you believe in. It's important to do your homework, too, because expertise counts. People are more likely to be persuaded by someone who really knows what she's talking about. Showing respect for others, is always a good idea. Isn't it nice to know that respectfulness is very persuasive? People don't feel manipulated or taken advantage of when they're treated with respect. Finally, there's a persuasiveness about being professional; dignified, knowledgeable, and careful not to waste others' time. These personality attributes will be their own reward, but it's comforting to know, too, that sincerity, fairness, warmth, energy, expertise, respect, and professionalism will help you to succeed in persuading others to appreciate your point of view and act accordingly.

Again, it's *their* thoughts and actions that you want to influence in persuasion. The actions and thoughts still belong to them, not to you. Persuasion is not power over someone; it's power with someone. The skills we're talking about here are skills that will put you in the most effective position to convince them to change a thought or action, but not to force that change. Because it's power with someone, there are two in the conversation, and one terribly important part of persuasion we haven't thought about yet is what's going on in the other person's mind. You can only know that if you ask and listen to the answers, then respond to whatever concerns, needs, hopes, and fears the other person has shared with you. To be certain you've heard them correctly, it's important to ask questions to clarify, to give feedback, to check your ideas about what they are thinking.

If they have doubts and hesitations, are not ready to go along with what you want, then the best thing is to ask questions about the doubts, and reassure them with your answers. For example, if you want someone to plan a picnic with you Saturday, and they think they may not have time, ask if there's anything you could do to help them free up the time—maybe study with them sooner, so the homework is all done. Maybe they're afraid it will rain; you could have a plan B for rainy days—maybe a picnic under a shelter in a pretty spot. Unless you listen and take their concern seriously, you don't have much of a chance of persuading them, no matter how logical, warm, expert, and so on you are.

OK—here's a fun "assignment", homework. Why don't you each try to persuade a friend of something special to you? Then, ask that friend to rate how you did on logic, empathy, character, the personality traits of sincerity, fairness, warmth, energy, expertise, respect, and professionalism, and on good listening. Each time you do that, your skill and effectiveness will improve. It's definitely worth the effort, because people who are persuasive have lots of other people helping them achieve their goals, making for good company and good progress!

Workbook Questions:

1. Rate yourself on a 1-5 scale on the personality traits needed for persuasion: sincerity, fairness, warmth, energy, expertise, respect, and professionalism.
2. Why do you think character is more persuasive than logic?
3. Rate a persuasive person you know on the traits in question 1 above.

Managing Your Time Well

- Steps for managing your use of time
- Learn to live "on purpose" more of the time
- Experience "flow", living fully in the present

Do you sometimes feel really pressured, as if there just isn't enough time? Have you ever felt guilty when you did something you enjoyed, because you knew there was something else you thought you should be doing? And have you ever felt as if everything depended on you, and on getting everything done? Lots of people have these unpleasant feelings, and it's from being out of control when it comes to managing time. Actually, we can't manage time at all—it comes in regular, measurable chunks, and we can't stretch or shrink it, or affect it in any way. It's kind of funny, the way we talk about time—saving it, for instance. Where do we put it when we save it, under the mattress? What we can manage is ourselves, and the ways we use our time. Some people do that much more effectively than others, and so it seems as if they have more time than others as a result of their skill, but we all have the same 24 hours a day to work with.

Of course we know exactly how much time we have in any given day, but none of us knows how much time we have altogether. No one has a contract that gives her so many years of life; no one even knows for sure that she will wake up alive again tomorrow. Since the total amount of time given to us is an unknown, we might wind up with much less than we expected, or much more. I believe we must treat each day as our most precious responsibility, the tool we have to achieve our purpose here on earth. I'm not talking about keeping busy, for busyness is not the same thing at all as meaningfulness. In fact, you could say the people who are excessively busy are hiding from life, rather than living it. To fully live each day, to best use each 24 hours entrusted to you, it's necessary to live with purpose. Steven Covey, the author of First Things First Every Day, says in his subtitle, "because where you're headed is more important than how fast you're going", and that sums it up beautifully. It means that living with purpose, even when the pace might seem slow, is far more useful and satisfying than a whirl of busywork that may mean nothing at all in the long run. So the first lesson is to be certain of what's you're trying to do with your life. If you're irritable, short-tempered, and tired, maybe it is a warning to re-think that purpose, and get back on track.

In addition to living "on purpose", we need to live in the present. Many people live in the past, always talking about the way things used to be, or the way we always did it. Others live in the future, telling you what they are going to do, going to be, going to say next time. But the only time we can actually live is the present, right now. The past is wonderfully useful for lessons, and the future is equally useful for inspiration, motivation, and dreams, but real life happens right now. We need to fully be where we are, pay attention to what is going on right now, and live completely awake in the challenging, fearful, glorious now. That's one secret to rich, full living—to squeeze every drop out of the experience of each moment, and share that experience with people important to you. Many authors talk about the amazing phenomenon of flow, of being "in the zone", of losing yourself in your activity of the moment, whether it's basketball, writing, painting, thinking, reading, creating a budget, or anything that takes all you've got. It's a celebration of being human, taxing skill and concentration to the limit, and rewarding the effort with a feeling of being on purpose, just right, fully alive, and satisfied with life. That's what living fully in the present can do for and with you!

Another principle for managing yourself in your use of time, in addition to purposefulness and present-centeredness, is to work on being organized. That doesn't necessarily mean being neat, it means knowing what you have to do and having the needed things readily at hand to do it without distraction or interruption. It also means making a list where you identify what's most important. Don't worry about identifying what's most urgent—you can't avoid those things, like a ringing telephone, even though they may not be important at all. Being organized helps you overcome indecision, which is one of the biggest time-wasters of all. When you're organized, not only do you feel more self-confident; others will have confidence in you as well. One secret to organization is to figure out when your peak periods of time are each day, and put your most important activity into those blocks of time. It's like having an extra day or two a week! Peak periods are those times when you're really alert, sharp, curious, and capable, as opposed to the times when you're just there, like after lunch, when most people are barely awake. Peak times aren't always under your control—maybe you have a class scheduled then, and can't do your own thing, but sometimes you can control those peak times, and it's very productive to do so.

We've been talking about how best to use your time. I'd like to say a word about respecting the time of others. If you often interrupt someone, perhaps your Mom, maybe you could instead write down the questions and ask several at once so you interrupt her less often. You know how it distracts you to be interrupted; it works that way for others as well. Purposeful living in the present, with enough organization to be effective and with respect for others is the very best use of that wonderful resource, time, that I know of. I wish you a long life filled with many, many days like that.

Workbook Questions:

1. Rate your home and work areas on organization—can you find anything you need in less than one minute?
2. Do you know when your "peak periods" are each day? Try doing a puzzle every two hours or so until you find the time period or periods when you are at your best, and then put your top priority action items into that time slot.
3. List two ways you can improve your use of time, starting this week.

Becoming a Team Player

- Teamwork has advantages in nearly all aspects of life
- Most Americans are trained for individual effort and reward, not for teamwork
- 5 simple rules for top performance on your team

I was so proud and excited about being a cheerleader in high school, it never occurred to me that I could have been on the team. Girls didn't do team sports then, we just got to cheer the teams on. So, we never learned whether we had what it takes to be team players. In fact we never learned what, exactly, it takes. It's taken a lifetime to figure that out. Mostly, I've messed it up. But when it works—Wow! You feel so powerful, so very good at what you're doing, so in tune with everybody else, that it's practically an out-of-body experience. The level of trust, sharing, and caring rivals anything but Mom. What an amazing experience! At least, it's been extraordinary for women of my generation, who all had to learn about teams the hard way.

Things are different for the younger generation—you've been on soccer teams, and lots of other opportunities are coming your way. Do the coaches ever tell you that what you're learning on the field is good stuff to know in the classroom, and later on, in the boardroom? It's enormously important to learn how to be a good team player, as well as learning how to be a very competent individual. Mostly, our national heritage, history, and hero stories are about rugged individuals, people who succeed by their own brains and brawn. In school, we earn our grades by doing our own work, and if we share information, that's called cheating. So, we learn to keep it quiet. Then, we get to a job and the supervisor tells us we're not good team players because we don't share information. Go figure!

As frustrating as all this can be, the basics of being a good team player are pretty simple, even though they run against that individualistic grain. Listen to the coach, keep your eyes on the goal, forget about your ego. You're not here to be a star, you're here to help the team win. Stay in tune with the rest of the team, supporting the team publicly, keeping any quarrels and criticisms private. Those five principles will put your team in a winning position anytime you're reaching for a goal, whether the team is family, school chorus, church, work group, community, or nation.

Listen to the coach means first of all, not talking back. Recognize and respect the coach's wider experience, and understand that he or she may have reasons you know nothing about, which they can't share with you because of privacy, or the law, or just plain efficiency. So, listen. If things don't go the way the coach told you they would, wait until an appropriate time and ask questions in a respectful and tactful manner. Ask, "What should I do differently?", which will give the coach a face-saving way to make adjustments and corrections. There's no harm in being kind.

Keep your eyes on the goal means to be constantly aware of the purpose of the group or team. If it's to win games, then all the energy needs to go in that direction. Whatever the purpose of the group, stay focused on that and only that. It's so easy to get distracted, to waste energy on sidelines that don't pay off, to spin your wheels doing things that don't add up to any satisfaction or progress toward the goal.

Forget about your ego means to stop trying to show up the others on your team, and concentrate on helping the whole team achieve its goals. Teamwork is not a place to be looking for individual praise; it's a place to help the whole team score. The key word is contribute—if you can polish your contributions to the team and its success, you've made yourself valuable. Always remember that if you're bringing to the team value over and above what you cost, in time and trouble, your place is secure. The same question will go through your boss' mind when you're working later on—does she contribute more than she costs? People who don't, don't last very long.

Staying in tune with the others is harder to talk about, but it's critically important. Think of a pro basketball team, running down the court. One team member shoots the ball over to, not where the teammate is when he shoots, but to where he knows the teammate will be a split second later. How does he know that? Well, that's what tons of practice together and paying attention to each other's ways of acting in the game will do for you. Staying in tune also means providing back up for someone who's getting tired or hassled, keeping the whole team strong.

Supporting the team publicly means keeping disagreements private, and showing the world your loyalty. If someone has a criticism and wants your comment, just refer them to the coach for information about that. Talk about how proud you are to be a member of the team, and how sure you are that the goals are within reach. If you have a concern, take it to the coach in private. If you follow these rules, you're sure to be a sought-after member of any team you like.

There's a role for individual ability here, too, of course. To prepare for helping any team reach its goals, you have to develop your skills as well as your attitude. Practice is the only way to bring out all the natural ability you have. Practice is often a private thing, but to get really good at anything, you need feedback, and a chance to correct your mistakes. Other team members can help with that, and you can return the favor for them. Give the feedback to them with tact. Don't talk about how they "always" or "never" do this or that. They deserve a fair look at what they're doing right now. And when someone hands you some unwelcome criticism in the way of feedback, just ask yourself if they're trying to be helpful. If so, say thanks, and consider that there might be a little nugget of truth in what they tell you.

Teamwork isn't so hard, once we get that old prideful thing, ego, out of the way. I'm glad I've had a chance to experience some great teams, and I know you will, too.

Workbook Questions:

1. Think of some examples of good teams you've been a part of. How did the experience feel? How good were your abilities while a part of those teams?
2. Can you think of a time when your ego has been a problem for your teamwork? How could you have handled the situation better?
3. Why is trust important between team members? Between members and the "coach"?

Saying No Nicely . . . and Not

- The four-step method for saying no without losing the friendship
- How to protect your interests while helping others meet their needs
- Know when it's not necessary to be polite, but rather to just protect yourself

Girls used to be raised to be "nice", to behave cooperatively at all times. Often that meant that they had a hard time refusing people who wanted them to do something, even if it was something they'd rather not do. I thought things had changed a lot, but in my seminars women often tell me they still have a hard time saying no to other people's requests, even when they were too busy, or not at all interested. So, when I found a way to talk about saying "no" nicely, I thought it was well worth sharing. It's a 4-step process, and it's doesn't work unless you do all four steps.

Suppose a person you don't know very well calls to invite you to her birthday party next Saturday. While generally, you like going to birthday parties, you were hoping to go hiking with another friend that day, and you'd really rather keep your day open in case you can do that. So here you are, on the phone, wishing you knew how to say no without hurting anybody's feelings. Has that sort of thing ever happened to you?

Step one in handling this problem is to really listen to the request. Often, we think we know what someone's going to ask, and it turns out that they wanted something else instead. Part of good listening is asking questions, so you might ask the caller what time the party is, and about how long it will last. That way, the person calling you is sure that you have given your full attention to their request, and that you fully understand it.

Step two is the hard one, but it's only step two out of four. Steps three and four will make it work out well for you almost every time. Step two is to refuse the request—to say "no". It's usually better if you say something like "I wish I could", or "Darn, I'm not going to be able to do that". I call those weasel words—easier ways to say no, and they work very well.

Step three is to give a general reason. Examples are: "I've already made other plans", or "I have a conflict then". Don't give the exact reason, which in this case is, "I'm waiting for someone else to call to see if we can go hiking". The exact reason is often insulting to the person who is making the request of you, since it tells them someone else is more important to you. That may very well be true, but there's no need to say it and hurt their feelings. The general reason works quite well.

Step four, which really pulls the whole thing together, is to give the caller an alternative, another way to get what they want. In the case of someone who wants you to help celebrate their birthday, you could say, "Happy Birthday! I'm busy Saturday, but could you have lunch with me Monday, my treat?" That way she feels satisfied that you care about her birthday, and you still have protected your Saturday so you can go skating with your friend.

Sometimes for step four you have to think of other alternatives, like someone else who could substitute for you. For example, you might ask if she intended to call Sophia and invite her, and say, I know she'd love to go to your party! But only say it if it's true. You might think of some other way to meet the person's need, like sending an email card, so if she wanted to show that you care about her birthday, she'd have something to show her other friends.

Those four steps—listen, saying no, giving a general reason, and providing an alternative, make the process work almost every time. What you're doing with this system is protecting yourself and helping the other person to meet their need—a very advanced skill called assertive communication. Don't be surprised if it takes a lot of practice—most adults aren't very good at it, and they've been communicating a long time! You have a great advantage if you can set up practice sessions with friends. Just ask to borrow money, or some other request, and see if they have learned how to say no nicely. Then turn the tables, and gently refuse a request of theirs. Give each other feedback on how well you applied the four steps.

Once in awhile, you'll get a request that is so inappropriate, so rude, that saying no nicely just isn't the right response. Someone might be asking you to try drugs, or allow touching that is out of bounds, or cut classes with them. In cases like that, there's no reason at all you should worry about protecting their feelings—just say no—loudly, firmly, clearly, and quickly. Then walk away. You have a "free pass" to be as rude as necessary to protect yourself. In case the person asking is a friend and you're surprised to see them acting this way, you can use a little more diplomacy—say something like "I'm surprised to hear something like that from you!" You'll probably keep the friendship that way, but if you don't, they're headed in the wrong direction, and the friendship isn't worth it until they turn that around. Maybe you can be the one to help them get turned around, if you're strong in your own beliefs and actions, and caring towards them.

If someone does make a request of you that makes you very uncomfortable, try handling it the way I've suggested, then talk it over with someone you trust. With their help, you may be able to prevent that person from becoming a predator who harms others selfishly.

Workbook Questions:

1. Do you generally have difficulty saying no to unreasonable or unwanted requests? How do you feel when you give in, even though you don't want to?
2. Why is it important, when saying no, to try to offer the other person a way to meet their needs while protecting your own needs?
3. Try practicing this system in artificial situations, such as with a friend, pretending to ask for things you don't want to give, so that the skill is available to you when you really need it.

Understanding Girl Talk and Guy Talk

- Guys and girls, men and women just don't speak the same language
- Neither communication system is better; they're just different
- Knowing how the other gender communicates protects you from misunderstandings and avoidable conflicts

The last time we saw each other, your Aunt Eileen was teasing you about boys. It's the first time I've seen you both blush and admit that there are a couple of special boys that you know. Isn't it fun? It made me think that I'd better write you a letter to talk about some of the basic differences between the way boys talk and think and the ways girls talk and think. I hope this will save you some confusion, misunderstanding and heartache in the future.

There are a lot of people who have made it their lifework to study the differences in thinking and acting between men and women, and fortunately for the rest of us, they've written some very helpful books. My favorite authors are John Gray, who wrote books like *Men are from Mars, Women are from Venus*, and Deborah Tannen, who wrote *You Just Don't Understand*. Neither of these authors believes that either males or females are better, they just have different ways of expressing themselves. I'm not sure exactly when these differences show up, but I remember my girls being different in behavior from my boys very early in childhood, and I imagine you can see some of these things I'm about to explain in yourselves and your friends.

Let's talk first about some of the behaviors that are different in communicating. Girls touch each other more when they're talking, maybe to brush something off a shoulder, or put a curl back in place for someone else. Guys usually touch each other only to wrestle, push, congratulate, or tease each other—have you noticed that? When girls are talking, they move closer to one another, and they like to face and look at each other, but guys would rather be further apart, standing or sitting more side-to-side and looking around. You'll see that girls move their hands more in the air when talking, and guys tend to keep their hands down or behind them. Of course, there are exceptions to all of these observations, but they are generally true. Take a look around the the places you go everyday, and see if you can pick out these differences.

Both John Gray and Deborah Tannen, as well as others, say the main difference in conversation between men and women is that men, and probably boys too, are trying to figure out who's in charge, who's "top dog" in each situation. Women, and probably girls, are more into connecting with the other person, seeing what they have in common. In addition, they agree that males are more direct and straight-to-the-point more of the time, and females take more of a "scenic route". They say males try to lead, and females try to cooperate, which isn't a very good fit, so one or both are confused when they try to interact. It would work better if two people cooperated, or one led and one followed, since the two different ways of communicating don't mix very well.

Males and females use different words more frequently, and I'm not sure at what age that starts. For example, you rarely hear a man say the word "precious", unless he's talking about precious metals, nor do you hear him say the word "tummy" unless he has an infant, or maybe a stomachache. Women don't use as much of the rough, "blood & guts" language as men do, although there are certainly some who use it quite a lot. Women, and I'm guessing, girls also, answer a question with a question, and like it that way. If one says "What do you want to do today?", the other will say, "I don't know, what do you want to do?" If you ask a guy what he wants to do, he'll just tell you. That wouldn't be a problem, except if it was a girl asking, she was hoping for a question back so she could suggest something.

Girls also tend to respond to a compliment with a compliment. "That's a pretty sweater." "Thanks, I like yours, too." If you compliment a guy, he'll probably just say thanks and not pay you a compliment back. It's just the way they talk, so don't get your feelings hurt over it. Girls sometimes use tag questions at the end of a sentence. Those are little two-word questions they use in order to get a conversation going. An example would be "That's a really big Christmas tree. Isn't it?" Now, she knows whether it's big or not, she just wants a comment from the other person. A guy would not use the tag question, he would just say it's a big tree. The most common example of this type of thing is what we call Valley Talk in California, for the Los Angeles area, the San Fernando Valley, where supposedly it originated. That drops the tag question, and just puts a question mark after everything, supposedly to get a response. For people who don't talk that way, it just sounds slightly dumb. "We went to the mall? And there was this new skate shop? ", and so on and on and on. At best, it sounds insecure and very trivial, so please don't let that habit get started.

When people get old enough for jobs, these differences really can cause some problems. A woman supervisor, for example, might give an order that sounds more like a question, or a choice. "What do you think about helping Harry out?" A man supervisor would just say "Go help Harry.", but they both mean the same thing. You can see that it's important to always check with the other person. In this case, the smart thing would be to ask "Should I go help him right now?"

Although these differences may be changing a little as we all have more of the same experiences, they really are not changing very quickly. I'd like to make a couple of recommendations. First, entertain yourself by observing very closely some of these differences between guy talk and girl talk, remembering that neither is better; they're just different. Second, whenever you're talking with a guy, take an extra minute to be very clear, and to be sure you understand what their meaning is. Even though it sounds like you're speaking the same language, in some ways, you're not. It's part of the spice of life, and a delightful conversation topic all its own. Enjoy!

Workbook Questions:

1. Try a brief conversation with a friend of the opposite gender, using the body language described above, and see what happens. Then, switch roles, using each other's body language style. How does that feel?

2. Watch a group of males or females interact, and write down how they stand, whether they touch, and so on. Do you think you would be comfortable acting as they do?

3. Why do you think males and females talk so differently? Is it worth trying to change?

Learning to Lead

- Leaders are big-picture people, thinking more about why than exactly how
- Leadership technique has changed to become more inclusive and sensitive
- Leaders keep the goal in mind at all times, and communicate that goal often
- 8 steps to leadership excellence

When you see something that needs to be done and nobody else stepping up to do it, you volunteer. Other times, a teacher or boss asks you to be in charge of something. Either way, you're exercising leadership, whether you go for it, or it's handed to you. I'm sure you've had chances to experience this already, and it will happen over and over again throughout your lives, so let's talk a little about what this leadership stuff is. It's one of the most widely written about subjects in both politics and psychology, and still, it's not perfectly understood. What is known, however, is that lots of people would like some of it, because the rewards are pretty great. Besides the power, the prestige, the money, and the fame that often go with leadership, there's the interest and satisfaction factor. The old saying is that "The scenery only changes for the lead dog". That's sure true—the leader gets to see what's out there, ahead and around the corner, and the others only get to see the leader's backside! When we moved to Mexico, Captain Bob drove the truck and towed the boat and I followed in the car. He got to see the beautiful scenery of California, New Mexico, Sonora, and all the other lovely places we passed through, and I got to see the back of the boat.

Leaders are the big-picture people; they see what needs to be done, and why. Sometimes the followers don't understand or appreciate this, because they're too busy with the details. Those details may turn out not to matter much at all, like arranging the deck chairs in neat rows on the Titanic. Leaders welcome ideas and participation from everyone, of course, but they're not afraid to shout: "Forget the deck chairs; man the lifeboats!" when that's needed.

People from very different points of view have been writing about leaders for all of human history, and they agree on at least one thing: leaders are the people who get things done, and that hasn't changed. From Hannibal crossing the Alps on elephants to a rock star raising money for AIDS treatment in Africa, leaders always have gotten things done. What's new is the emphasis on how they get those things done. Today, the method is nearly as important, and sometimes more so, than the results. In general, successful leaders today are those who pay attention to the people on their team, as well as to the team's goal.

So, whether your leadership experiments are with the soccer team, a classroom project, a job, a community organization, or something else, it will help to keep that double focus from the beginning. Here's how. First, don't just listen to the ones making the most noise. Include everybody's ideas in your thinking and discussions. The people who are just a little different may have the most creative ideas. Second, ask people to support any suggestions they have with facts, success stories, and other information so you can evaluate the idea properly. Third, re-state the purpose of your group as often as needed, so everybody stays on track. Fourth, show, rather than tell, how to be responsible, focused, dedicated, and respectful. Fifth, if your group makes a mistake, acknowledge it and ask what you've all learned from that experience. Sixth, when you choose a solution, keep an open mind about it, for it may not be perfect, and might need some fine-tuning later on. Seventh, protect your group from outside pressure so they can concentrate on getting the job done. And last, give people things to do that interest them, stretch them, and help them grow. You want your team members to get really good. Remember, a second-rate leader surrounds herself with third-rate people, but a first-rate leader surrounds herself with first-rate people. Grow some first-rate people, and you'll always have a top-rated group. This kind of supportive, goal-focused, respectful treatment makes people want to help you succeed, and keeps them loyal to your group or team. You'll be glad you did it this way.

Where you are, right now, is a good place to start practicing to be a good leader, attracting those opportunities you want. There are two ways to prepare, and this is a good time to start. The first thing is to pay attention to building competence, just getting good at doing things. While you're doing that, also pay attention to how you learned to be good at those things. Knowing how to learn is a highly sought-after skill now, because once you get a job, whatever you've learned in school to prepare for that job will be out of date in no time, and you'll have to keep learning very quickly. People in my business seminars have taught me, one way to stay on top of an area of knowledge or skill is to keep a notebook, looseleaf or on the computer, so it can be updated constantly, as things change. Add to that a group (it's fashionable to call it a network) of capable friends who can be counted on to help keep you up to date, and also add a commitment to lifelong learning, and you can keep that skill highly polished.

The second way to prepare is to keep improving your emotional intelligence, a term Daniel Goleman uses to cover such things as adaptability, persuasiveness, initiative, and empathy. Those qualities; being flexible, being persuasive, being willing to jump in and take the lead, and understanding and caring about others, are even more important in today's work world than IQ, according to some very solid research he's done. Unfortunately, the evidence is strong that people of your generation are steadily losing ground in this area of emotional intelligence, becoming more depressed, worried, angry, nervous, and generally emotionally troubled than previous generations. That's distressing. If there's to be a solution, and I'm confident there is, it will come from you and others like you.

The issues your generation will face are huge; global warming, the spread of nuclear capabilities, poverty, disease, crime, pollution. It's not too soon to start growing leaders to face these issues, and you are well equipped to be in that very special and very much needed group. Start exercising these leadership skills now, so you'll be ready.

Workbook Questions:

1. Describe the best leader you've ever known. How are you like that person?
2. Do you think leaders need emotional intelligence? What happens if they lack it?
3. Which of your leadership opportunities so far have been most satisfying? Why?

Resolving Conflict

- The positive potential of conflict
- Five powerful conflict resolution strategies and when to use them
- How to stay objective and oriented toward problem-solving

Do you ever get really, really angry with each other, or with someone else in the famly? Do you ever have hurt feelings that just don't go away? My sister and I used to drive our parents crazy with our constant squabbling. It's funny how the people you care most about can hurt you the most. But conflicts can, and do, crop up anywhere—at school, at work, in the family, with friends. They're just an inevitable part of life, since we don't think alike, don't see the world the same way, and don't want to give up our hopes, dreams, and chances for someone else with a different agenda. I've been lucky, not to escape conflict; I've had my share—but to work with many leaders and many groups on preventing and solving their conflicts. I've found some great resources and some very useful ideas, and want to share some of them with you to smooth your path as much as possible, so you can save your energy for better things than fighting.

First, we need to acknowledge that conflict can be horrible, but that it doesn't have to be. It can sidetrack energy, widen differences between people, hurt morale, and cause people to act in ways Miss Manners would call "regrettable". When handled with skill, however, it can be highly educational, for it clarifies issues, releases emotions, brings about honest communication, gets people involved, and increases the chances that a solution will be found. Samuel Johnson speaks for many when he celebrates the clash of ideas that brings advances: "I dogmatize and am contradicted, and in this conflict of opinions and sentiments I find delight." (Life of Johnson, p.92). The difference is that in positive conflict, people approach the issue with skill in search of an answer; while in negative conflict, people approach each other to do harm so that they may win.

Some conflicts, however, have no positive potential, and should be avoided to save your energy. Don't argue with someone who is overly emotional, is on drugs, or drunk, or attacking you instead of the issue, and is dangerous to your safety. In those cases, walking away is the better part of wisdom. The rest, you can reasonably look forward to with some excitement, for you're bound to learn something!

One of the first things you'll learn is that people have very different histories with conflict, and very different skill levels. Some have never heard of a win-win resolution, and wouldn't know how to start to achieve it. Personality style, too, plays a part. The more aggressive people go on the attack, while the less aggressive look for a way out. If you're faced with an aggressive opponent, maintain your confidence, and do your best to listen carefully, and then to be heard. Counter any interruptions calmly, saying, "I wasn't quite finished". You will do well to set a tone which says "We're really both on the same side, here, trying to solve this problem."

For a wonderful resource on ways to keep that tone going, check out the book *Tongue Fu!* by Sam Horn. It gives you a number of ways to disarm hostility and move conflicts into cooperation.

One of the hardest skills to develop, but well worth the effort, is to keep conflicts objective. That means, to aim at discussing with the other person some issue or problem, not what's wrong with that person, and not what's wrong with you. You can look at the problem from their point of view, invite them to look at it from your viewpoint, and generally keep the destructive emotions out of the discussion if you can focus on *it* rather than on the personalities involved. In order to do that, you'll have to control your urge to blame the other person, and you'll have to prevent yourself from speaking those angry thoughts that you're thinking. Stay calm, stay objective, and the problem pretty much takes care of itself.

I mentioned that's it's OK to avoid some problems, when the other person isn't rational. I also believe that in some cases, it's OK to suppress, or shove under the rug, certain kinds of problems. That technique is only useful when the subject isn't one you're ever going to agree on, and the relationship is important to you. That's when a truce, agreeing to disagree, is essential.

While there is a role for avoidance and for suppression, the strategy most aggressive people like best is simply winning. However, they never think of the drawbacks—lost opportunities to learn, and lost relationships with those who have been on the losing side. Given that high price tag, the only time I would recommend going for a clear win is if it's an ethical issue, or if life or safety is at stake. Otherwise, use either compromise or cooperation.

Compromise is useful to get things moving, and it's probably the best technique of all when the subject isn't too important, like where shall we stop for lunch on this trip? If it's a big deal topic, however, compromise will leave everyone feeling a little cheated, and it's better to just invest the time and trust and effort in working out a cooperative, creative solution. That's a really high skill level, and not many people have arrived at it. But with practice of the ideas and principles I've mentioned here, you'll be in a very good position to find cooperative solutions to your conflicts, and to maintain the relationships with the others that you'd like to have, so you both win.

Let me give one example. Let's say you want to sell your old Bronco, and there's a teenage boy in the neighborhood who wants to buy it. You're asking $1500, but he only has $1250. You can't lower the price, because you need the money for kitchen remodeling, so you ask his family over for lemonade to discuss it. Once you explain what you need the money for, the mom says her brother has a lumberyard and might get you a better price on your kitchen work, so you're closer to a solution. Then the boy volunteers to mow your yard and walk your dogs until he's earned the difference. He gets the car, you get the kitchen remodel, your dogs get walked, your lawn gets mowed, and the mom's brother gets a contract. Not bad. That's how good conflict resolution works—everybody's happy, and they all got something they didn't even know was possible when the conflict started. I know you're at least that creative!

Workbook Questions:

1. Which strategy—avoidance, suppression, winning, compromise, or cooperation—do you most often turn to? What might work better in some of these situations?
2. How well do you usually do at keeping conflicts objective? What could be improved?
3. Think of a time when you cooperated to solve a problem and everyone gained. What keeps you from using that skill more often?

Chapter 3

Things That Get in the Way

Anger

- Learn how to use the energy "rush" of anger in a positive way
- If something makes you angry, it's because you care—that's good!
- Habitual displays of anger shut down communication from others
- Anger management is a set of readily available skills, building on simple strategies like "time-out"
- Learn tactful, understanding responses that prevent confrontation from escalating

This is an odd topic, I know, but I'm trying to help with important and difficult subjects, and this one is a doozy. For starters, everyone gets angry, but as a society we pretend that only wicked people get angry, and in their out-of-control emotionality, they do terrible things. There isn't even a polite way to express anger. So here we have a little guilty secret that troubles nearly everyone, a universal emotion that no one seems to know how to handle properly.

Let's start by admitting that anger has its good, and useful, side. First, it tells you that you really care about whatever the subject is that has your blood boiling. If you don't care about something, are truly indifferent to it, it just can't make you angry! Secondly, anger presents you with an impressive burst of energy—lots of power to fix the problem, make a change, or solve a difficulty. But all we usually do with that energy burst is throw something or yell. So, again, here's a secret—a resource at our disposal, if only we knew how to use it.

Third, anger is a very complicated thing. Sometimes it's connected with jealousy, with guilt, with frustrated wants, with fear, and with hurt. Sometimes it comes on quickly and sharply, other times it's more like a slow simmering. People have different levels of "normal" anger, the attitude they carry around all of the time. Those who are often impatient, frustrated, on their guard against being cheated, expecting bad things to happen, feeling watched all the time, those people carry a high level of anger, and it doesn't take much of an event to cause an explosion. Still others who are usually sad, jealous, resentful, disrespectful of others, insecure, and have feelings of worthlessness, also carry high levels of anger.

We know from medical research that making a habit of angry feelings is very unhealthy, leading to many potentially deadly diseases. Not only is habitual anger horrible for your own health, it's tough on all those around you, too. They will tiptoe around you, or avoid you altogether, fearing that any attempt at honest communication will trigger a war. They feel cheated out of a good relationship with you. People who cause this reaction in others have a harder time getting hired, are rarely included in invitations. They aren't sought out for leadership positions. And since they are ready to blame others for everything, they just take their isolation as proof that everyone's against them. What a sorry existence!

One sure sign of out of control anger is a temper tantrum. Have you ever had one of those? Did it help make the problem better? Probably not, if my experience is any guide. When I was little I had quite a temper, and my cousin Jack, a little younger than me, was often the victim of it. One time I even put him in a wheelbarrow and threw it off the garden wall! Well, in spite of my temper, Jack survived and grew up—way up—he became over six feet tall. One summer not long after we were grown, I visited him at the family's cabin in the Adirondack mountains, and he was so nice. He took me out in a canoe. Of course, half way across the lake, he stood up. That's an impressive sight, a six-footer standing in a canoe. He started to rock, and said very sweetly: "Linda, remember that wheelbarrow?" Was that lake ever cold! It seems it's true that what goes 'round comes 'round, and your behavior comes back to bite you!

If you ever, in anger, feel as if you're going to do something as foolish as throwing a person off the garden wall, maybe it would help you to know that there are some pretty fool-proof ways to manage anger. The most widely known, of course, is the time out. Count to ten, take a break, develop a sudden coughing fit and have to go get a drink of water. Give yourself some time to get your emotions back under control. There are some other tips just as useful. Ask yourself how important, in the long run, that thing that's making you angry is. Will it matter terribly five years, weeks, or minutes from now? Getting some perspective helps you calm down. You can remind yourself that the person who is behaving in a way that you respond to with anger is probably doing and saying what seems best to them at that time. People can only behave in ways that are consistent with their knowledge and their desires, so maybe trying to understand that person's information and wants will help you be more compassionate and less angry.

Another very powerful strategy for managing anger is to strengthen yourself so that you're not so vulnerable to it. Take good care of your body, use mini-relaxations to help you think more clearly and less rigidly, practice meditation or prayer frequently, and set your mind on positive things to crowd out the negative.

Each and every time you find yourself becoming angry, stop and calmly decide whether you're going to allow that emotion to take control of your life, even for a few minutes. If the decision is no, then have some well-practiced, considerate responses ready to deflect the anger, both yours and the other person's. You might say, "My experience is different", or "You may be right, at that", or "I can see how you might feel that way". None of these commits you to their viewpoint, nor do they insult the other person. If you decide that you want to experience and use the energy that anger gives you to make a bad situation better, then use all your skill for that purpose, rather than for destructive ends. In the long run, you'll be proud of yourself, others will be impressed, and you'll be developing rapidly in wisdom and understanding.

Workbook Questions:

1. Have you been angry in the last week? The last 48 hours? Are you satisfied with how you dealt with that?
2. If you wanted to take a "time-out" to calm yourself and think, would storming out of the room accomplish that? Why or why not?
3. Do people with a "chip on their shoulder" have healthy self-esteem?
4. What's the best example of anger management you have seen? What's the best strategy you have used, yourself?
5. How can you turn anger into fuel for accomplishing your goals?

Stress

- Stress is a sign of life, not a sign of importance
- The 5 best stress management techniques
- Learn the secrets of hardy people

How many times have you heard people say, "I'm so stressed", as an explanation or an excuse for their poor behavior? Lots of folks think a high level of stress is a sign of their importance, and complain continuously about the stress in their lives, mostly to impress others, or to justify behavior that isn't good for them, like drinking or spending too much. There's so much publicity about the evils of stress that you'd think it was a matter of life and death! Actually, it is, in extreme cases. All of the major killers, including heart disease and cancer, are connected with out-of-control stress. And, well before it gets that bad, there are often symptoms of stress, like anxiety, backaches, neck aches, headaches, depression, frequent colds, fatigue, bursts of anger, lots of mistakes in your work. Different people react to high stress in different ways, of course. The more aggressive people tend to go on the attack, and the less aggressive people tend to avoid the situation that caused the stress as much as possible. Neither approach solves the problem, and may in fact make it worse. So, high levels of stress can certainly be unbearable, even fatal.

In spite of all this, I'm a fan of stress, as long as it's at the right level. You see, stress is a sign of life. You need a little stress to keep you moving, interested, and capable. Without any stress, or anxiety, or tension, you're sleepwalking through life, not tuned in at all. Having the right level is like being up for the game, or being ready to stand up and give a report in class or committee. Sure, there are butterflies in your stomach, but you can learn how to make them fly in formation. The right level of stress produces high energy, mental alertness, calmness under pressure, thorough analysis of problems, improved memory, sharp perception, and an optimistic outlook. See why I'm a fan?

Here's what happens when you get your stress level to work for you rather than against you: stress hits you; you think of and use a strategy for handling it; your strategy works; you see yourself doing well; your view of yourself is improved; you get stronger. You'll find yourself dusting off your hands and saying, "Bring on the next one!"

Unfortunately, if you don't know any good stress management strategies, the picture is a lot different. Stress hits you; you try a strategy like yelling or running away or drinking; the problem is not solved, and your poor strategy may create an additional problem; you feel the stress overload symptoms I mentioned earlier; you get sick. The difference, as I'm sure you have figured out, is the kind of stress management skills you know and use. Here are a few of the very best ones I know about. They are mostly ways of keeping yourself strong, calm, and ready to solve problems well.

First, know the most important thing you have to accomplish each and every day. Whatever else you might have to give up doing that day because of interruptions or changes in plans, try very hard to get that top thing done. That keeps you satisfied with your progress toward your goals, and the stress you experience doesn't make you feel overwhelmed. Second, take care of yourself with nutrition and exercise. A healthy person is in much better shape to handle sudden stress, and to be able to remember tools like listening, speaking calmly, problem solving, and so on. Third, nurture—that means take good care of—your relationships with friends and family, listening to them as much as you talk. Those relationships form a solid support group when you are under a lot of stress, and you can go to them to reassure you and to help. Fourth, take care of yourself mentally. Build up a positive attitude, have plans and goals for your personal growth, spend some time each week doing creative things, relax frequently, even if only for a few minutes, and don't take responsibility for problems you didn't create. These things keep you sharp and contented, to be in the very best position to handle stressful emergencies. Fifth, and finally, make a point of succeeding at something important to you each and every day. Those last two strategies will keep you flexible, positive, and mentally strong. All of those qualities are powerful in keeping stress within levels that don't harm you. While none of us can prevent stress from showing up in our lives, we can be prepared to meet it and manage it effectively.

Since those strategies should be something that anyone could learn and use, isn't it strange that some people seem to easily conquer stress while others are crushed by it? There's a body of research known as hardiness studies that has investigated these differences. Hardiness refers to people who are not easily destroyed by problems. They tend to bounce back, they are survivors. These people, according to the research, share four qualities that the other people don't seem to have. They are connected to others; that is, they cherish their friends and families. They seek challenges, not looking for the easy way around in life. They like to learn and practice enough to have some control over areas of their life, and they keep looking for ways to make those areas larger. Finally, they serve something larger than themselves. They are committed to their faith, or to principles, ethics, or values that are very meaningful to them. They are terrific models for all of us, showing us how powerful connection, challenge, control, and commitment can be.

Remember that high levels of stress can come from positive things as well as negative things. In one well-known rating system, getting married is considered to be more stressful than getting fired! I think it's because marriage brings on changes in every area of life, where if you find a new job right away, you may not have to change too many other things, even if you lose a job you've had for awhile. You could stay in the same house, for instance, and you'd see the same people around the dinner table. So, when something good happens to you, it might be quite stressful as well as quite wonderful. The stress management skills I mentioned in this letter will be helpful then, just as when something unfortunate happens. Remember, it's true that stress is a sign of life. If you're living as fully and deeply as I hope you are, there will be lots to manage.

Workbook Questions:

1. What do you usually do when you are under stress? How well does that strategy serve you? What might be better?
2. Hardiness studies say the 4 C's are important—connection, challenge, control, and commitment. How would you rate yourself on these qualities?
3. List three stress management techniques you could be using more often, and more consciously. Try to increase your use of them over the next few weeks, and keep track of the results.

Depression

- Reasons why women are more prone to depression than men
- Strategies for avoiding and overcoming depression
- Distinctions between sadness and depression

Think of this letter as preventive medicine. Knowing what's in it will be like taking your vitamins while reading up on why vitamins are good for you. Because depression is so common, I expect that you will soon know, if you don't already know, a friend who is suffering from it, and perhaps one day it will threaten you as well. From 8-11, more boys than girls experience depression, but from then on, the rate for girls rises rapidly until, in adulthood, women are twice as likely as men to suffer from it. Let's talk a little about why that is, and how you can protect yourself, and what to do if you or one of your friends is experiencing depression.

First, though, I need to clarify that being sad for a good reason is not depression. If your pet dies, if your science project gets broken, if your best friend mistakenly thinks you said something bad about her, if someone dear to you moves away, the feelings you have of sadness are perfectly normal, and will soon go away. Depression is a much deeper and longer lasting sadness, often coupled with feelings of worthlessness, blaming yourself, and having no desire to go on living. For children, there are four things that seem to go with depression: being a victim of bullying, using marijuana, drinking alcohol, and having eating disorders. I'm not sure you're familiar with eating disorders, but they involve things like thinking you're way too fat even if you're skinny, and eating a lot, then making yourself throw up, and doing that over and over again. Gross, yes, but also terribly dangerous. For teen girls, body changes are also sometimes seen as a cause of depression, because people around the girl have mixed feelings about her growing up, and she gets confused about the messages she's getting. The hormones that cause the body changes contribute to depression in some cases, as well. None of that is anybody's fault, it's just a problem that needs a solution.

So there are lots of reasons why it might happen, and by the time people are adults, about 18.8 million Americans, or over 9% are clinically depressed, and still more, about 35 million, or 16% of the population, seek treatment for depression sometime in their lives, according to the 2003 study of the National Institutes of Health. It happens more often to people whose parents or sisters and brothers are depressed, and for women, the hormone changes with pregnancy and giving birth might trigger the disorder. Most serious depression, though, is found after some major life stress, like sexual abuse, or other violence. It happens more frequently for people who dwell on symptoms of distress, thinking of them over and over. In the worst cases, it leads to suicide, even in young people, so there's good reason to recognize it and help the person get treatment right away.

There are medications that doctors often prescribe for depression, and in about 2/3 of the cases, they work pretty well. Other forms of help include meditation, relaxation, exercise, and some herbs, such as St. John's Wort. At school, and often at work as well, there are counselors available, and they will know which treatment is best for which situation where there's depression. You can recognize some of the early symptoms, or signs, of depression. The person sleeps a lot more than normal, and seems not to want to get involved with anything or anyone. People who are depressed are withdrawn, and seem to shut down, trying not to feel anything at all, because their feelings are so unpleasant.

If you or a friend ever feel this way, take a good look at what you're thinking, because thoughts cause feelings. Challenge the incorrect thoughts, by refusing to take blame for things you didn't cause, by taking credit for good things you did cause. Plan to work at preparing yourself so that you don't give up on things too early or too easily when you're trying to reach a goal. Go to a counselor, or someone else you can trust, and let them know how you're feeling. Another important step in prevention is to keep yourself healthy, especially paying attention to good nutrition and exercise. And finally, don't try to control every single thing. Some things you should just walk away from; they're not worth the effort

For girls and women, the major danger area for feelings that cause depression is, much more than anything else in life, their relationships. Relationships with parents, relationships with friends, relationships with boys, and then, with men, this is the path where she's likely to slip into the sad, self-blaming pit of depression. Especially if she sets high standards, and holds herself responsible if the relationship doesn't meet those standards, she's likely headed for a fall.

In his excellent book, *Undoing Depression,* Dr. Richard O'Connor talks about how depressed people think everyone knows the secret to happiness except them, and that they get too tangled up with the people they care about, not knowing where that person stops and they begin. Then, if something goes wrong, as if often does with relationships because we're human, the letdown is terribly painful. By concentrating on where we stop and others begin, so that we know what our responsibility for our behavior is, and what thoughts, feelings, and choices are ours and what ones belong to the other person, much of the wrong thinking that leads to depression can be avoided. In the most simple terms, if you stick to your business of becoming your best self, and enjoy connections with other people who are busy becoming their best selves, there's very little chance either of you will ever have to climb back out of depression, because you won't be in danger of falling into it in the first place. But, just in case it ever threatens, keep these ideas and encouragements handy—your life is too precious to spend time in this kind of misery.

Workbook Questions:

1. When something goes wrong, do you usually blame yourself? What other factors might be in play?
2. When something goes right, are you able to take credit for your part?
3. How does building connections with friends and family help prevent depression?

Guilt

- Guilt may be a sin of pride—not everything is your responsibility
- Ways to separate actual failings from imagined ones, and act to repair and restore
- The steps to overcoming guilt and making amends

There's a hole in my heart. Into it stream all the accusations, and out of it pours all the guilt for so many things done and so many things left undone. Some days I can't breathe for the weight of it all. Had I done something differently, perhaps divorce would not have happened, John might have lived, and Alan, too. Brian might have come through in better shape, Eileen wouldn't have been so angry for so long, Michael's schooling might have been paid for, Nancy might have flourished without my bossy big sister self in the way. Maybe even mom would have lived, if my furiously independent teen ways had not added so much stress to her life. If I had visited dad more, he might have eased into Alzheimer's more slowly. If I had not been concentrating so much on my studies, my work, my career, would things have been easier for my children, my pets, my friends? If I had kept the house cleaner, would the neighbors have liked me better? If I had worked harder in the church, would fewer divisions have happened? If I had campaigned harder, would better people have been elected? If I had given more, would there be fewer poor? If I had recycled more, would the world be cleaner? I should have been more humble, more giving, more supportive of others. I would have taken the time, if only I had known. I could have lived a different better, more wholesome and fruitful life.

Some of that is true, and some of that is just silly and stupid. I get confused about just what I'm responsible for. The "if only's, should haves, would haves, and could haves" of life convict me, and they convict us all. But—and thank God there's a but—that's not the whole truth. Oh, there's plenty to feel guilty about, all right. When I find myself getting angry at someone because my conscience is pinching me, there's an indicator. When someone's criticism stings and I get defensive, there's another. When I'm feeling just a little paranoid, there's another, for as Shakespeare said, "Suspicion always haunts the guilty mind: (Henry VI, part 2). When I know that something is wrong, and do nothing, I am at fault. When I know better and say nothing, there is no place to hide from my accuser. So, there is enough true evil in me to wear my knees out begging forgiveness.

But there is, as I said, more to it than that. I am not, after all, in charge of the universe, nor am I in charge of other people's decisions and actions. Taking responsibility and feeling guilty for those things is simply an ego trip, making myself out to be more powerful than I actually am. This kind of guilt is in itself a sin of pride. I need to limit guilt and responsibility to my own thoughts, actions, and inactions. Unfortunately, that still leaves plenty of clean-up work to do.

When I have violated a law, or a moral standard, or when my brother truly and righteously has something against me, then I am condemned, and there is work to do. Some of that work is mine to do, and because I'm Christian, I know that the largest part of that work has already been done for me. Being guilty of something just makes me part of the human race, for all have sinned. Not doing my share of the clean-up, however, makes me twice guilty. The steps in acknowledging the error and seeking pardon are clearly laid out for us.

The first thing I have to do is search my heart to find those things that I am responsible for and have failed in. The second thing is to acknowledge and confess those failures. The third is to make amends to anyone I may have harmed. The fourth is to turn away from such actions or inactions in the future, and the last step is to replace those actions with more righteous actions. By accepting the grace of forgiveness, and by disciplining my self to change my behavior, I am freed of the convictions, and the guilt is gone. It's just gone. I was guilty; I am pardoned. I was bound, I am free.

It's like cleaning your room. Done, but you know you'll have to do it again, and soon. Nevertheless, for the moment, it's done and I am at peace. The horses grazing outside my window don't shy away from me, the hummingbird drinking from the bouganvilla by the fountain has accepted my presence. I am not accused by the neighborhood dogs who come for a handout, nor by the gardener, nor by the tenant upstairs, nor by my husband, who should know. So for just now, the evil in me is at rest and I am thankful. Maybe I can remember for a little longer this time who I really am and who I am not, and that will be enough.

Workbook Questions:

1. Do you sometimes feel guilty for things over which you have no control? Can you begin to work on letting go of that inappropriate guilt?
2. Is there someone you need to make amends toward? How can you begin to do this?
3. Why does accepting forgiveness need to be followed by changed behavior?

Difficult People

- People who are obsessed with their own issues strike others as insensitive and difficult
- We are all potentially difficult to those who differ from us
- Assertive communication and careful listening prevent many difficult situations

Someone asked me the other night at a party what technique I would recommend for getting rid of someone who wanted to be friends more than he did. My first thought was, what a nice problem, to have too many friends. But I know his question was serious, and that there really are some folks that are a bit hard to bear. At that same party there was a woman I had thought would make a good new friend, for we have some things in common, but she was so loud, so strident, so insulting to other people's opinions that her sobriety, if not her sanity, was in question. How disappointing. And then, just yesterday, I had a visit from a lady I've wanted to get to know, and she answered four cell phone calls while we were trying to talk, and after each, made critical comments about the caller. I guess now I'm afraid to be her friend, for fear of what she might say about me after we've spent some time together. Difficult situations, difficult people; they seemed to have cropped up a lot lately, so I'd better write to warn and support you, in case these things happen to you, too.

I'm sure I've been a difficult person, and probably pretty frequently, for difficult people are those who are so full of their agenda, their goals, their ideas, that they barely notice you and certainly don't take time to listen to your perspective. Over the years, there have been lots of times when I've been pretty forceful about my goals, which had the positive outcome of achieving them, and the negative outcome of maybe being difficult in the process. So, the first bit of wisdom I've gleaned is that most people don't start out trying to be difficult. They mean well, if they think of it at all, but their interests, obsessions, fears, depressions, hurts, and needs get in the way. If they see you as blocking their route to whatever it is they want at the moment, you become the enemy, and they are contentious, angry, spiteful, contemptuous, and hurtful. Add to that the fact that few people of all the billions in the world have had any communications training at all. Most just speak as the thoughts occur to them, with no effort to clean it up, make it palatable, add a tactful introduction or summary, or otherwise show any consideration for others. So far, I've said that difficult people are tactless and self-centered, ignorant of better communication techniques, and so obsessed by their own agendas that they wouldn't be interested in learning them if the opportunity came along. Whew! Makes you want to stay home in bed, doesn't it?

Then, add to that the amazingly different and creative ways in which we can be difficult, and you'll see that the problem threatens to grow out of control. Our personality types, our histories, our birth order, our gender, our culture, our age, and our religion all exercise some constraints on our behavior, and guide our expressions in certain paths, and away from others. Let me give a few examples. Take an adult US white male, somewhat technically oriented, probably of an analytical frame of mind. Others might see him as difficult because he's slow to make decisions, not necessarily very sensitive to people's feelings, or insists on being the expert who has the last word, and is always right. Another person, let's say a lively, personable female singer, might be seen as difficult because she loses important paperwork, is sometimes late to appointments, and doesn't always follow through with plans, or listen carefully to others. Yet another, older, manager-type person might be seen as too bossy, and his secretary, as too weak and compliant. We all are potentially difficult to those who are different from us, particularly in moments when we're thinking about what we want instead of about communicating clearly and successfully with the other person.

So what tips and techniques do I have to offer you so you can safely get out of bed and go through the day, knowing you can handle the difficult encounters awaiting you out there? I've been hinting at them all along. Recognize that the other person has his or her own goals, agendas, and style, and that those things are unlikely to perfectly match yours. So, listen carefully, ask questions, offer summaries so they know what you think you heard, and encourage them to give examples to clarify things you aren't sure of. Whenever you honestly can, honor their knowledge, and always honor their experience. At the same time, honor your own. Say things like, "My experience has been a little different . . ." Ask what they want to accomplish, and listen to the answer. The person who asked me about getting rid of a troublesome friend really wanted to protect his own reputation and integrity, and didn't want to even tell a white lie to let the person down softly. Knowing his goals helped me shape my response to his question, and made it more difficult. But I liked him better, for few people are willing to take risks to protect their integrity.

For most difficult encounters, your good communication skills, particularly careful listening and speaking assertively, not aggressively, about your point of view, will minimize the problems. Using "I" language to prevent any perception of attack also works wonders. I might have said to my visitor, for example, "I'm finding it hard to concentrate on our train of thought when the cell phone keeps interrupting." For some situations, when the other person is being fanatical, or is not sober or sane, your communication skills won't help, you just need to get away safely. Those encounters are not beyond the realm of possibility, but rare enough to generally believe that most of the time your skill will create a positive, or at least an enlightening, outcome. You may solve the problem, and you will learn something, and probably keep the relationship intact. Not bad for a little exercise of discipline.

Workbook Questions:

1. Think of three people you consider difficult. Are they alike, or quite different from each other? Why is that important?
2. Do you think others sometimes consider you to be a difficult person? Can you change your communication style a little to reduce this impression?
3. Try the exercise of careful listening and feedback with a person you consider to be difficult. Note any change in the relationship as a result.

Jealousy

- Insecurity is the root of jealousy
- How to challenge your feelings of inadequacy
- Deflect envy, and compete only against your own high standards

Mary and I were sitting on the porch at camp one summer afternoon and she was telling me about packing to go away to college. Her dad owned the gas company that my dad managed, and our camps were next door to each other at Green Lake, in the Adirondack mountains. My pink plaid shorts and pink t-shirt were pretty clean, and I almost had picked the scab off my knee so my legs looked OK. I was surprised she'd take the time to tell me about her plans. She was older, prettier, and much richer, and I could hardly stand it. When she said she was taking a trunk with fifty-two sweaters in it, mostly twin sets, I nearly died. Twin sets were all the rage, and the prettiest girl in my class at school had several that I would have loved to own. It seemed as if everyone had them but me, although I think I had one or two. It was a beautiful day, the lake was cool and clear, the little sailboat was waiting, my cousin Jackie would have been ready to race across the lake, or to go water skiing with me, but all I could do was pout about those sweaters and what I didn't have. How silly it seems now, but the pain was real then.

That pain, like all jealousy-caused pain, really comes from insecurity. When you feel that someone has something that you don't, whether it's a nice smile, a good grade, a cute boyfriend, or a fancy car, your insecurity is telling you that (a) you don't deserve to have something like that, and (b) maybe you could have had it if only that person hadn't gotten in your way. So, you begin to dislike that person, perhaps spreading rumors about her, and pretty soon, you find yourself laughing when she stumbles, hoping she'll just disappear from the face of the earth, leaving all the good stuff for you. Sadly, jealous people really do not wish others well, instead, they hope those others will fall from grace and lose their advantages in the fall. And, by focusing their thoughts on that other person, they avoid dealing with their underlying insecurity, which caused the jealousy in the first place.

Freud, who founded psychology, thought women were naturally jealous, as well as envious, and felt shame, inferiority, and that they received pleasure from being dominated and embarrassed. What a relief that not many psychologists still carry those ideas around, but they don't deal much with the whole concept of jealousy, either. The only place it seems to come up is in marriage counseling. By then, I think, it's pretty late to be treating insecure feelings that have been troublesome for many people since at least grade school.

When you're feeling jealous, I believe the root cause is in insecurity, but more precisely, in two ideas about inadequacy. First is the belief that you're not good enough, don't have enough talent, beauty, intellect, or whatever, to be worthy of the thing you want. Second is the belief that there's not enough of that thing to go around, there's not an adequate supply. So if someone else gets it, you can't have it. Remember, ideas cause feelings, and feelings lead to actions, so it's important to look at the ideas behind your feelings and see whether they have any merit. In this case, I think these two ideas about inadequacy can usually be challenged successfully. The belief that you are just not good enough can be challenged by clearly defining the standards of "good enough", and seeing whether you want to work hard enough to meet those standards. Since most of us operate way under our full capacity, there's plenty of room for growth, if we decide to work at it.

The second idea about inadequacy, that there's just not enough of the prize to go around, may or may not be true. If the prize is a certain guy named Jake, then it's true that there's only one, and if Suzie has his attention right now, he's not available to you. However, he might be later on, or another guy may come along who is even more interesting, once you work yourself up to meeting those higher standards you decided were worth it. Or if Suzie has been accepted at a top college, but you haven't, maybe you could try again, or go to another school and transfer later, or just decide to become a top student at that other school. It's like dessert; yes, there's only eight pieces to this pie and once they're gone, they're gone. But who says you can't bake another pie? So, jealousy could stimulate you to do some needed self-improvement, and in so doing, you'll be too busy to pout about those jealous feelings, and you'll be leading an interesting life, too.

It's a little bit of a different story when the jealousy is directed at you. That's very painful, even though some think it's a compliment. California's current Governor, Arnold Schwarzenegger said, "Everybody pities the weak; jealousy you have to earn." I don't think it's a prize, I think it's very uncomfortable, and can cost you friends. Because it stems from that person's insecurity, their feeling of inadequacy, it's hard for you to directly respond to it, except by building them up whenever you honestly can. Humility helps here, too, and reflecting the envy away from yourself. Attributing any success to hard work also helps, for then the jealous person can see that if they choose to work hard also, they might be able to do what you can.

One evening some friends were over and asked me to play piano for a little while. I played a Beethoven Sonata that I had been practicing daily for several months, and it is a very lovely piece. At the end, one of them said a little too loudly that it was beautiful, and how much she wished she could play like that. I was quick to pass the compliment to Beethoven, mentioning how incredibly brilliantly it was written, because I just don't think playing piano is a competitive sport for me, but rather a source of enjoyment. What had sounded like a jealous comment on my playing became a delightful discussion of types of music we each enjoyed the most, and the evening passed comfortably. I don't mean that you should never accept compliments; of course you should, with a genuine "Thank you". I simply mean that you should never encourage envy. In my way of thinking, we're not competing against each other, but rather against standards that we set at the highest level we can. We're the only person in that race, so jealousy has no place.

Workbook Questions:

1. Under jealousy is the pain of insecurity. Think of a time you were jealous, and try to identify what you were insecure about. Now challenge that insecurity with facts.
2. Do you agree that "jealousy is something you earn"? Why be proud of something that badly affects your relationships?
3. How can you use your feelings of jealousy to set higher goals for yourself?

Impatience

- Useful techniques for developing more patience
- There are lessons in the waiting
- Yield control over all but yourself

Does it sometimes seem that you spend half your life waiting? Waiting for something to start, waiting for car or computer repairs, waiting for a friend to come over, waiting for Christmas. Common wisdom says that patience is a virtue, and the Bible says "In your patience possess ye your souls" (Luke 21:19), but it sure is more natural to feel impatient, isn't it? After all, you have a life to live, and waiting feels like wasting time.

Before your Dad was born, I had a pottery and weaving shop, where I taught classes and sold my artwork. Some of the weavings were tapestries, pictures in yarn and other materials. There were two lessons for me in the weaving of tapestries. One was about patience—each little bit seemed so small and insignificant, and yet they all, after many, many hours, added up to a meaningful whole. The second lesson came after the whole weaving was finished. From the top, the creator's side, I could see the design clearly and usually it was satisfying to me. However, from the bottom, all anyone could see was a mess—bits and pieces of colored yarns, ends sticking out, nothing that made sense. A popular sermon story about that time said God's handiwork was like that—he could see the design of our lives, but all we saw was the mess—ugly little end pieces sticking out, and nothing that looked like it was supposed to be that way. Without the right perspective, and trust and patience, life can be very discouraging.

Patience implies a total control of yourself and it acknowledges a total lack of control over everything else. It requires waiting, waiting for someone else to act, waiting for the weather to change, waiting until you're old enough to drive, waiting until the doctor calls back with the test results. And very few of us are any good at all at waiting. We fidget, squirm, and try to micromanage the universe. I've found a few ideas that relieve the impatience a bit. Some of these ideas are more helpful for short waits; some for the big stuff that seems to take years.

When you just have to endure something for a little while, there are a few techniques that are very useful for increasing your patience. One powerful technique is to think of something wonderful that's going to happen later on, after the not-so-pleasant experience you have to endure. For example, when I had a lot of dental work done, I often found the patience to sit for hours in the dentist's chair by thinking the whole time about what fun we would have when you came over later that week! Because no brain can do two opposite things at once, deliberately thinking about something nice can squeeze out the negative stuff, and give you a sense of patience and peace. Another technique is to keep your mind blank, to just rest it and be still. You might count to 10 over and over, or say the same nonsense word or words over and over. When a distracting thought interrupts, just say hello to it and let it go away while you continue counting. It sounds too easy, but it's not easy, and it does produce a quiet that gives you patience.

Impatience is natural when you're young and eager to get on with your life. When you think about the long, long years of school, and the waiting to get married, get a job, and have kids, all those things that make for independence and adulthood, I know that it seems it will never happen. The best cure for that sort of impatience is just to put one foot in front of the other, and keep doing that day after day. It's disheartening to try for a distant goal, but the little piece of that goal that you could accomplish today, why, that's in your sights, and you can do that! So do it, and tomorrow, do tomorrow's part, and soon you will be near your goal, wondering where all those wonderful years of youth went.

In most cases, this step-by-step approach is very effective, but not always. As Violet Fane remarked long ago,

> Ah, "All things come to those who wait,"
> (I say these words to make me glad),
> But something answers soft and sad,
> "They come but often come too late."

It's true, we don't know the future, and we can't predict whether what we're waiting for will ever, in fact, come at all. I've found that the way to maintain my sanity and not yield to the evils of impatience is to distract myself with something productive. To take an example that's close at hand, we're entering into what I call the "sweaty season" in Mexico, the long, wet, hot summer. Without a purpose and a productive activity, my disposition would deteriorate as quickly as the humidity rises. So, I'm playing music for our church, practicing diligently all week, and writing these letters to you keeping active and positive as best I can. Since I can't control the weather, nor rush the coming of the beautiful Fall season, I have to put my energy where it's likely to make a difference. In the satisfaction of these productive efforts, in the very doing of these things, there's a comfort, a yielding to the flow of time, a sort of patience after all.

Workbook Questions:

1. What do you find it hardest to wait for?
2. How would setting daily goals help you become more patient about big projects?
3. What one thing could you stop trying to control, so you can use that energy to gain more control over yourself?

Change

- Understand the predictable process of change
- Learn to support others in their anxiety and anger during change
- Become more aware of the constancy of change, and of the different response times each person has

When my parents were young, nearly everyone lived a very stable life, with very predictable expectations and events. People grew up in the community where they were born, went to school, sometimes only through fifth or sixth grade, helped out at home, got a job, learned how to do it well enough, and then either stayed with that job the rest of their lives or took a promotion and stayed there for years and years. They married, almost always only once, had a few kids, and after forty or so years of work, they retired and helped out at home again, maybe living with one of their children. That pattern sometimes happens now, but it's much rarer. Now, people move around a lot, go to several schools, sometimes working for awhile before they go on for more school, get married and quite often, divorced, maybe more than once, have some kids, and change communities and jobs very, very often. One study I read said that the average job now lasts only 3 years, instead of a lifetime. Even though you're not working yet, you still experience change—you take vacations, your family structure changes, you have homeschool, then go to public school, you get the flu, then get well, new friends move into the neighborhood, money comes and goes, you have a fight with your sister, your beliefs get challenged by things you're learning, and many, many other things happen. That's a lot of change!

When changes happen in people's lives, they go through some very predictable stages in response to those changes, and not all the stages are pleasant. I guess that's why people generally don't like change. But, without change, there would be no new medicines, no air conditioning, no cars, no jazz, no computers, no electric ice cream makers. Without change, you wouldn't be learning new things or growing up. It's not that change of itself is good or bad, it's just that most of us don't know how to handle it well. There are some pretty good guidelines that I'd like to share with you, both to make your experience with changes more understandable and satisfying, and to give you the skills to help friends and family members who are experiencing some rough changes.

The first thing that happens, especially with changes you don't think you're going to like, is that you try to pretend it isn't happening. You might really believe on one level that it is not happening. That's called denial, and it's very common. The only problem with that is part of your mental energy is busy holding the truth away from you, so you get tired more easily, and you can't concentrate as well. Eventually you become aware of the truth about the change; that it's really happening, and if someone is responsible for telling you that, you might be angry with them for spoiling your fantasy that everything was staying the same. In fact, you might just get angry, period. Anger is one of the common reactions during the second stage of change, which is called resistance, because you're fighting it. Resistance might also come out as confusion, or just not caring, or feeling that you're not you anymore since you can't do what you used to do, because of the change. Resistance is pretty ugly, and you can't think very well during this stage. It's hard to get much of anything done, but with support, you can pass through this stage into the next one, which feels much better.

Stage three is called exploration because you're just learning about the new situation caused by the change. You don't yet know how to function well in the new circumstance, but at least you're willing to try. Here's where a good teacher, mentor, or coach can be a lifesaver. With their help, or with just a lot of trial and error struggle on your part, you make it through this stage to the final stage of commitment to the new situation, to the change. You'll feel better, be more active, get more done, and be more cheerful. But don't be too smug—here comes another change, and you have to go through all the stages all over again! It's like being in whitewater—lots of waves of change all the time, and you're in different stages with each one, and everybody around you is experiencing their own series of changes. Not a smooth ride, but an exciting one—just think of whitewater rafting and you get the idea.

Those are the stages in a nutshell—denial, resistance, exploration, and commitment. Everybody's in one of those for every change going on in their lives. Believe me, we could all use a little understanding and help with this rough ride. People crave three things during change, and you can be a great help to them if you try to provide a little of those things. They want *empathy*, or understanding that it's a painful process. They want *information* so they can see what's going on and what's coming next. Finally, they want some *useful ideas* from people who have already done what they're trying to do. If you can provide any of those, you're a good and helpful friend. More specifically, if they are in resistance and being angry, you can just hear them out. If they're experiencing confusion, maybe you can help them set a clear direction. If they're worried about not being the same person anymore in the new circumstances, you can point out that they still have that wonderful sense of humor, or ability to fix things, or whatever consistency you can see. And if they are just worn out and disinterested in making it through the change, you can offer encouragement and hope. All of us would benefit from friends who knew how to do give those gifts at the right time.

We can't avoid change, nor would we want to, although sometimes we all wish we could. Already today, my schedule has changed three or four times, priorities have shifted, income and expenses for the month have been adjusted, and there have been many other little and not so little changes. I'll bet your day hasn't been all smooth sailing, either. These changes are all signs of life, and knowing how to best handle them is an important tool for living the good life.

Workbook Questions:

1. Name one change in your life that's going on right now. What stage are you in- denial, resistance, exploration, or commitment?
2. Why does someone get angry when someone else tells the truth about change, forcing them out of denial?
3. Think about two people close to you, who are experiencing a change similar to yours. Are they in the same stage as each other? As you? How can these people help each other?

Money

- Why money doesn't buy happiness
- How we use money to measure worth, and the pitfalls of doing so
- Learn whether the 80% rule will work for you

Filthy lucre, it's called. And it's said that the love of money is the root of all evil, but don't we all love it still? Who hasn't dreamed of rolling around in a vast bin of it, tossing it into the air, playing Scrooge or Santa Claus with our millions? I've had a lot, I've had a little (a lot is definitely better), and along the way maybe I've learned what it is that we can and can't do without, and why money is such a complicated thing for all of us. "Render to Cesar that which is Cesar's", Jesus said, marking the stuff as the province of this world. But just to cover all bets, we put "In God we Trust" on ours, in case the next world should be looking. And what televangelist doesn't shout the loudest when telling you, not asking you, but telling you to send in all you can spare. No wonder we're confused.

Ask anybody how much they need, and they'll usually say that a little more than they have would be about right. No wonder there's such unhappiness. People at all income levels feel that they don't have quite enough, but families at every financial level suffer from the same proportions of debt, abuse, alcoholism, and other ills. So there is ample evidence despite our craving for more, that money in fact cannot buy happiness. What it buys is more comfort in which to live our lives, happy or unhappy that they may be. But the money itself doesn't produce the happiness or unhappiness, rather the way we live does that.

While it may not guarantee happiness, it has its uses, that's for sure. In addition to providing purchasing power for food, clothing, and shelter, money has great psychological value, especially, but not only, in our culture. It pretends to offer security, and it is how we keep score as to who is important and who is not. Let's take the idea of security first. As long as we live, we will need food, housing, and other comforts such as medical care. These things are increasingly expensive, so we buy insurance to provide them in the event we are unable to work, and we lay aside some funds to help provide these things when we are too old to think about going back into the workforce. But the price tag of the insurance increases more rapidly than our income over the years, so when we most are likely to need it, it's out of reach, and the costs of care for an elderly person also escalate faster than we can save to provide for those costs. Frustrating, isn't it, how elusive the security promise is? Even though the habit is ingrained, I'm beginning to question the wisdom of laying aside treasure on earth after all. And don't get me started on social security—the government's obligation to let us have the monies back that we were forced to contribute over our working life. The brochures they distribute when you sign up are filled with threatening language about how many ways they can reduce or eliminate your benefits! So there's precious little security there, either.

Now, about the keeping score part, which for many Americans is their favorite sport. Ask anyone from another country, and he or she will tell you that an American can't have a conversation longer than three minutes without mentioning money, the cost of something, or someone's wealth. We are truly obsessed with, or possessed by, the subject. Many of our friends in retirement are struggling with identity crises—now that they don't have the big incomes to boast of, they wonder who they are. Once the big check stops coming in, the slavish customer service at the best stores stops as well, and the waiter who always saved you the best table has to be reminded of your name. Devotion to money is slavery to a love that may very well abandon you, sooner or later.

So what is the healthy way to think about, and live with, this confusing but necessary substance? One of the best formulas is the 80% rule. Live within 80% of your income, whatever that is, and save 10%, and donate 10% to others in need. The idea of living within our means seems like a fantasy to many, which is why there are credit counseling services cropping up all over the place. The poet e.e.cummings put it this way: "I'm living so far beyond my means that we may almost be said to be living apart." Unfortunately, that's a common, and dangerous, situation.

I like to think of money as a tool for getting things done. If I invest wisely, more can get done. If I want to make a donation, for example, I could offer a matching gift—they only get it if they can raise an equal amount elsewhere. That way, the beneficiaries work hard, someone else has the pleasure of donating as well, and there is twice as large a gift to achieve the noble aims of the organization. Or, I've used a tool called a Charitable Trust—I make a cash gift to the church, or another organization, but in the form of an annuity that grows each year so that the longer I live, the more they will receive when I eventually die. Such tools are everywhere now. For the daily needs, I have no more wisdom that any other coupon-clipping, clearance-rack scavanging shopper, but those things have worked pretty well over the years. I've been quite happy following the motto to never buy anything that isn't on sale. My weakness has been, rather, to buy almost everything that is on sale, whether I need it or not, which is a whole other subject.

At your age, and for many people much older as well, money is still a little mysterious. I'd recommend reading a kids' money column in print or online to take the mystery away, at least a little. When you're working, use the company-provided savings tools—they will usually match what you put aside—to get a head start on retirement income. Watch interest rates, keep an emergency fund in cash in the bank or in short term CDs, and ask, ask, ask questions until you are satisfied that you know something about how to use this tool. Keep some funds and some credit in your name when you marry, and don't be shy about keeping a close eye on the family budget. Be informed, be a little aggressive, and don't be afraid; it's not really filthy, and using it for good can be great fun!

Workbook Questions:

1. Write your monthly budget and try re-writing it using the 80% rule.
2. If we didn't so readily measure people's worth with money, what other tool could we use? Wisdom? Leadership? Others: _____
3. Why do you think that people at all income levels have about the same proportion of debt?

Chapter 4

Becoming Who You Really Are—a Lifework

Personality Styles

- The 4 basic personality styles are inborn and durable
- Each style has its own deep need, communication style, and way of expressing anger
- Boost your ability to get along with people of all types

Isn't it wild, how some people are always fun to be around, some are always quiet, some are very outgoing, some very shy? Each is pretty consistent, quite predictable, and very different from the others. You two have rather different personalities, and I'll bet you've noticed that your friends are not all like each other, either. One of the reasons that people go into such different kinds of careers is that their personality styles are so different, and it is natural to want to do different kinds of work.

Ever since the time of the ancient Greeks, people have noticed and written about the fact that individuals have very different personality styles. These styles seem to be inborn, and last most of a lifetime. The Greeks noticed four main styles, or types, and we also think there are four general types, although we call them different names and explain them differently than the Greeks did. If, as I suspect, the styles are pretty evenly distributed, that means about one-fourth of all people fit more or less in each category. This matters very much, because it means that roughly three-quarters of the people you might see on any given day are basically different from you, When you talk to them, they don't immediately understand what you're saying, and if you should complain to them that someone is treating you badly, they'll be inclined to tell you to shape up. The other one-fourth are more like you, and understand you pretty well when you speak to them. If you complain to them that someone is treating you badly, they'll sympathize, and say they would have done just what you've done, and it's true, they would have. The point is that if three-quarters of the people you will interact with are very different from you, it would serve you well to understand those differences, and how to best work with each of the personality types.

One type, or style, is quiet, gentle in disposition and very people-friendly. These people are kind, warm, caring, supportive, and helpful. They don't shout much, and don't insist on their own way. The usual term for them is Amiable, which means likeable. Good careers for amiable people might include nursing, child care, teaching, or some kinds of counseling.

A second type is also people-friendly, but a lot more noisy and lively. These folks are generally called Expressive, because they express themselves pretty forcibly. They are fun, talkative, colorful, life-of-the-party types. Good careers for expressive people might include sales, show business, elective politics, and maybe courtroom lawyers.

The third type is quiet like the Amiable, but not as people-friendly. They are more interested in tasks, in facts, in information. They are usually called Analytical, because they tend to analyze things a lot. They are reliable, cautious, thorough, and they don't take unnecessary risks. You'll find lots of them in computer science, math, banking, and most of the sciences.

The final type is also interested in tasks, and they are forceful like the Expressive, but more focused on goals rather than on people. They are called Drivers, and they are often found in leadership positions because of their determination to get the job done. These people can be counted on to persist in a task, whatever the odds, and they probably are most of the people mentioned in your history books because of their achievements. Others sometimes think they are pushy, so they don't always have a lot of friends.

One of the better books about all this is called *The Platinum Rule*. You know the Golden Rule, of course, which says to do unto others as you would have them do unto you. The Platinum Rule takes that to a higher skill level, and instructs you to do unto others as they would have you do unto them; because they are not just like you. In short, "Different strokes for different folks." What you have to gain by learning this is an incredible boost in your ability to get along with people of all types. If you want to do a project with an analytical type, for example, joking around will just annoy them. They want slow, steady, precise work which is neat and well-researched. The opposite type, the expressive, would probably appreciate some humor and a quick, attention-getting project with some flashy graphics. The amiable will probably go along with whatever the others working on the project want, but they will have to listen to her carefully to get the benefit of her good ideas; she won't insist on being heard. The driver will just take over and bulldoze their way to the end of the project, but if you can convince them that there's a better way, they'll listen.

One of the easiest ways to tell which kind of person you are talking with is to notice their pace, their speed. Expressives and Drivers move and talk more quickly; Amiables and Analyticals move and talk more slowly. Then notice their level of interest in other people; Expressives and Amiables are very interested in people;

drivers and analyticals are more interested in things, goals, and projects. Another sure way to tell is to notice what a person does when they are experiencing difficulties, and are stressed. The more aggressive types, the Expressive and the Driver, tend to attack, to fight, to strike out at the problem or at others. The less aggressive types, the Amiable and the Analytical, tend to withdraw, to leave the scene of the accident, so to speak. If people don't understand that, imagine how irritating it is for a fighter to be in conflict with someone who withdraws—there's no resolution at all.

Now comes the fun part—try to guess which you are, which your relatives are. How about your friends—can you tell? How about your teachers, or leaders in the community? Learning to identify and work better with each of the four styles will make your life far more interesting, fun, and powerful. Enjoy!

Workbook Questions:

1. Which style do you think you are? Based on what evidence?
2. Can you think of a time when you gained a new insight from someone whose style is different from yours?
3. Is there a "best" style? Is there a "best" combination for a relationship? Why or why not?

Confidence

- Confidence is a strong leadership quality
- A simple template for building skill and confidence
- Acknowledge and develop your sense of yourself as capable

Before you read this letter, I'd like you to write down five things that you are really good at, and also write one reason why you know you're good at that thing. In other words, what evidence do you have? Then, please circle any of those things that you have become good at within the last year. Look at your list carefully. These are areas where you have strong self-confidence, and you have good reasons for that confidence. In all probability, at least some of these things are ones you have recently become good at, because you're learning new things all the time. Finally, pick three other people that are important in your life, and write down, for each of them, one thing about them that you have confidence in. How do you know? You're building a way of making good judgments, and looking for evidence, and recognizing that these things may change over time, all very valuable skills.

Confidence is a characteristic that separates successful people from those who don't do so well. Confident people ask for leadership roles and they get them. Confident people ask for help and they get it and use it to get better. Confident people inspire confidence in others, so they gain followers and supporters. Confident people smile more, sleep better, and generally live a more rewarding life. They aren't plagued with the fears and worries that slow others down, they just move on toward their goals. Because it's so critically important for successful lives, I wanted you to have some experience with it right before thinking about it, which is why I asked you to do the exercise in the first paragraph. With that exercise fresh in your mind, you can easily understand what it takes to build and keep on building the kind of confidence that sets you on that rewarding path. You need to practice a skill, use that skill, get some feedback about how well you did, make some corrections and adjustments, practice it again, and keep doing that. That's the standard way you get good at something. Then, to develop confidence, you have to keep at it until you know that you can perform at that level at anytime, and trust yourself to do so. You have to know what the competition can do, and how you look compared to them. If you don't like the answer to that, then keep practicing until you're even better.

That process works whether you're trying to play basketball, sing a song, ride a bike, grow a garden, climb a mountain, or raise a puppy. Practice, evaluate, adjust, practice some more, notice how well you're doing. That's the simple formula. Now, if you want to get even better and more confident, and do that faster, there's an addition or two to the formula. Addition one is to set higher standards faster. Let's say you can make one out of ten free throws in basketball pretty regularly. Now try for four out of ten, not two, as you practice. As soon as you can hit four regularly, try for six or seven. The second addition is for developing confidence in your ability and skill in general, confidence in yourself as a capable person. To do that, you have to face the things you are afraid of and keep heading toward your goals anyway. One of the wisest of American women, Eleanor Roosevelt, once said, "You gain strength, courage, and confidence by every experience in which you really stop to look fear in the face." It's not pleasant to face fear, but it is the fastest way to grow.

When I was a speaker, traveling and giving speeches and seminars, I wanted to get better at it very quickly, and so agreed to give a memorized presentation to the California branch of the National Speakers Association for their criticism and suggestions. I agonized over that, worked myself into sleepless nights and dangerously distracted driving, and nearly forgot what I wanted to say on stage in front of hundreds of my peers. I was terrified! But after that, there's never, ever been a speaking situation in which I was afraid—I was cured! I did OK, survived that, and now no audience seems threatening. Painful growth, for sure, but fast and solid growth nevertheless.

I said I did OK—that was deliberate. It's important to take credit for what you do know, and not believe that you were just lucky if you happened to succeed. Luck does sometimes play a part, but it seems to support those who are already working hard to be ready. There's an old saying that "chance favors the prepared mind".

I want to encourage you to build up your confidence. I wouldn't be totally honest, however, if I didn't mention the dangers of over-confidence, of being too sure of yourself. When I was learning to fly, I made my first cross-country solo, flying in wind that was too strong for my beginner's level of ability. I radioed in to the airport as I flew the final rectangular pattern before landing, and was acknowledged by the weather guy on duty, since they didn't have a flight control person working there. I hate to admit it, but I flew the whole pattern backwards, and landed going the wrong direction, right in front of a plane taking off. I had to jerk the little plane over onto the grass to avoid a collision, and blew a tire in the process. After I stopped shaking, I radioed the weather guy and asked him—get the way I spread the blame around—"How could you let me do that?—I'm a rookie!" He said I sounded so sure of myself that he never even looked up to see where I really was. I'm lucky I lived to be embarrassed by that episode. The moral of the story is that people can be too confident, or think they know things they don't. So, always rely on evidence, on past performance, recommendations, track record, whatever you can get your hands on to evaluate your own and other's readiness for performance.

Finally, a word about the importance of not only being, but also looking, confident. Don't fidget, don't mumble, don't shift your weight from foot to foot, don't twirl your hair, or say "like, uhm." every third word. You look and act confident if you sit or stand tall, look people in the eye, speak clearly, and keep your body still except for gestures that underline the points you want to make. Looking the part is actually a large part of the battle, because by convincing others that you know what you're doing, you convince yourself, too, and the chances are good that you'll have something to show everybody once all the distractions are out of the way. Now go show 'em what you've got!

Workbook Questions:

1. Look at your list of 5 things you are really good at from the first paragraph exercise. Are any of these things you can get still better at? How will you go about that?
2. Have you ever overcome fear to gain confidence? Would you do it again?
3. Think of someone who looks really confident, and try to analyze what they do to give that impression, in addition to whatever expertise they have.

Mentors

- Mentors speed your growth in specific skill areas
- Tested steps in establishing a mentor relationship
- Both mentors and protégés benefit greatly

You have family members and friends who love you, and you have teachers and coaches who help you learn new skills. Sometimes, though, you're going to want and need other adults who can guide, instruct, support, and help you grow in specific areas of expertise. Those people, who might have a close relationship with you for many years, are called Mentors. In Homer's classic story of Ulysses and his travels, Ulysses had a son he was reluctant to leave behind, and he found a teacher to care for him and train him to become a man. That teacher's name was Mentor, and it's been a mark of honor and responsibility ever since to become a mentor to someone who is learning.

Research has shown that all of the top businessmen and nearly all of the top businesswomen have had mentors to help them on their way up the ladder. Mentors help in personal life situations, too. When your Dad was growing up, he had a very difficult relationship with his stepfather. He solved that problem by finding a mentor, another teen's father, a doctor, who took an interest in him and allowed him to spend a lot of time with their family, learning, growing, and feeling valued. When I left university life to start a training and consulting business, I found mentors who formed my Board of Directors, and instructed me in many things that would have otherwise taken years of serious mistakes for me to learn. When companies and governmental organizations get serious about training a new pool of diverse leaders, they often create formal mentor programs to pass on all the technical, political, and social knowledge the new leaders will have to learn.

Suppose you want to learn to ski, or to understand budgets, or how to communicate better with people who are very different from you. Let's say you have seen someone who handles this skill very well, and you've admired that person from a distance and wished you could spend some time with them, learning what they know. The first step is to ask around, to see if others you trust share your high opinion of that person. In other words, check them out. They may have some bad habits you would not want to absorb along with the good information. But, if they check out OK, then it's time to ask someone to introduce you, or to introduce yourself, and pay a compliment and ask a few questions of that person you admire. Then, watch how they handle your comments. Are they too busy to pay attention to you? Do they brush you off, or do they seem kind and interested? If you get a green light at this stage, then, volunteer to help them out in some way, perhaps passing out programs or leaflets at a talk they're giving, or serving refreshments after a meeting they've led. Make it clear that you're going to help because you want a chance to learn more about the topic and their way of doing things.

After that, the relationship will continue to grow if you continue to make yourself useful. You'll meet people through your mentor that you might never meet on your own. Doors will open to you, and you'll have more exposure to opportunity than you ever expected, and it will come very fast. On your part, there's a lot more work involved, but the rewards are clear. On the mentor's part, there are rewards, too. There's the pleasure of helping someone learn the things it has taken them a lifetime to learn, there's more work getting done because of your help, and there's an even stronger reputation for them as an expert.

For a long time, the subject of mentors only came up occasionally in people's growth. Now, it seems much more common, and there's a good reason. In my grandparents' and parents' lifetimes, people generally got one job and stayed pretty much there for their whole working life. Just a couple of decades ago, the average job lasted 10 years. Now, it's more like 3 years. So, if you're going to be changing the type of work you do that frequently during your working life, you don't have time for a long training period with each change. You'll need someone to help you along. Often, the relationship with a mentor becomes very close, and lasts many years. There are wonderful benefits in that, of course, and there are also dangers. Sometimes the mentor tries to influence you in subjects outside of his or her expertise, and sometimes the relationship interferes with your dedication to your own family. Think carefully, and set up some ground rules together at the beginning, such as no weekend work, or always having a third party present at your discussions, to prevent those problems.

As soon as you have some expertise in anything you enjoy, consider becoming a mentor-in-training, and passing that information along to someone else. During your time together with that person, you'll find there are conversations about many things, and you'll have the opportunity to share your views on a wide variety of subjects. As long as you're not forcing your opinions on them, this can be very enjoyable for both of you. I think being a mentor is even more fun than having one, and there's no need to wait until you're much older to get started. A last word of caution. Be loyal, and respect confidentiality. Your character shows very much in mentor relationships, and your pride in your ethical standards should be your guide.

Workbook Questions:

1. Have you ever had, or been, a mentor? Was the relationship valuable?
2. What dangers do you perceive in a mentor relationship? How will you avoid these problems?
3. Suppose you have a good relationship with a mentor, and a friend or co-worker is jealous. How would you handle that situation?

Birth Order

- Life experiences are shaped in many ways by birth order
- Adults often carry behavior patterns learned as they fit into the family constellation into all their home and work roles
- Personality style and other factors may greatly affect the birth order role

There seems to be a pattern in the way older and younger siblings turn out. At work, first-borns tend to try to run things, a habit developed in their early experience. The younger siblings are more likely to be cooperative, peacemakers, team players. This very common and very visible pattern has exceptions of course, but it stems from some obvious limits parents face. There is only so much time, and when there's only one child, much of that time is available for him or her. When there's more than one, the time needs somehow to be divvied up, and not all parents do this well. My second daughter still reminds me that her baby book didn't have nearly as many pages filled in as that of her older sister. By the time I had four children, I'm sure all of them would have liked more individual attention that they were given. Like many parents, at least I hoped they were learning that the world did not in fact revolve around them!

Some of us are first-borns. What a kick to be first! To try everything for the first time, to test the limits, to enchant our parents, grandparents, and even the admiring passers-by. As Kevin Lehman points out in his birth order book, first-borns get a lot of the good stuff of life. Parents fuss over them, encourage them, and buy them educational toys. With all this attention and help, they tend to grow up fast, walking and talking early. They quickly become "little adults", achieving their way through school and later life. Many are strong-willed and pretty aggressive about taking life on and transforming it. If they want to know something, vague answers just don't work. They frown and ask again. If they want something, they keep at it until they figure out a way to bargain for what they want. Insistent, persistent, and pretty darn amazing—that's the story of the big sisters and brothers of the world.

People cut from this amazing and marvelous cloth are the first to learn that the world is exciting, huge, fabulously attractive and a little dangerous. They get to find out that they can't control everything, but often they try. Some develop something called perfectionism, wanting everything to be perfect. It may take a long time for them to learn that only the most important things in life deserve such high standards. And because they are role models for their younger siblings, someone is always watching, even though they would rather make their mistakes in private. On balance, it's a pretty good deal to be first, for there's always someone who thinks you're smart and able to handle life better than they can. That's a lot to live up to!

Because they've never been "the only", little sisters and brothers often learn to be more thoughtful, more considerate of others, and generally more giving. They need some time to develop their own sense of self, because there are some big decisions to make. They can choose to follow in their older sibling's footsteps, taking advantage of the fact that a trail has already been blazed, or they can learn to be manipulative, trying to make everyone feel sorry for them and give them what they want. There's a third choice, however, and it's both the best and the hardest. Younger brothers and sisters can decide for themselves what kind of person they want to be, and set out on that path, whether or not it's similar to the path of their older sibling. They can rely on their own strengths, develop their own friendships, and become their own persons. If they're lucky, and tactful and loving, there will still be that wonderful close bond with their brother or sister. When each person identifies, develops, and celebrates their own strengths, they all have the best of all worlds.

Workbook Questions:

1. Do you think your order in the family's children has affected how you act at the present stage of your life? For example, on a committee, would you lead or follow more comfortably based on your birth order experience?
2. Do you know people who are exceptions to the generalizations given here? Why do you think this happened?
3. For your own children, do you now, or do you plan to, try to counter the effect of their birth order, and if so, why?

Nobody Thinks Like You Do

- Ideas and values derive from life experience, which differs for everyone
- Conflict is inevitable and natural due to these differences
- Each person's unique thoughts lead to their unique emotions, actions, and impact

Sometimes something seems so obvious, but other people just don't get it! Has that ever happened to you? It's frustrating, maddening, and it's easy to think they are deliberately being difficult. Maybe so, but it's more likely that something else is going on. There are lots of examples that might help to understand what really is the case.

Although we're kind-of retired, you know I write, and have some piano students, and I try to stay involved and efficient. One day, as I was swimming laps to get my exercises done before two students showed up, their Dad rang the bell and there they were! I looked at the patio clock and it was still thirty minutes before their lesson time. So I mentioned that they were early, and said I would quickly finish my laps. I continued to swim for another ten minutes, then ran upstairs to get dressed for the lessons. Only much later did I find out that my patio clock had slowed and they were right on time—I was the rude one!

To explain how this kind of misunderstanding happens, let me share from one of the clearest thinkers of our time. In his book, *The Road Less Traveled*, M. Scott Peck says that the overall purpose of human communication is—or should be—reconciliation. For many people, this is a strange idea, since we usually think we're communicating to give or receive information, not to heal our differences. But he's right. The blunt fact of the matter is that our ideas are not shared, and cannot be shared completely. That's a big claim, so let me back up and lay some groundwork.

Where did you get your ideas, your beliefs, your values, your information? Isn't is true that you got all these things from family, friends, teachers, from all the sum total of your life's experiences so far? Indeed, where else could you have gotten those ideas, beliefs, and so forth?

And, further, isn't it true that others got all their ideas, values, beliefs, and so on from the sum total of their own life's experiences so far? And, finally, isn't it true that no two people, even those who are very close, can exactly share life's experiences? When you're horseback riding, you ride different horses with different levels of skill and success. When you're in school, you're in different classrooms. Sometimes you talk to a parent alone, sometimes you practice piano, or soccer, or basketball, alone, sometimes you eat a different flavor of ice cream, and you might have some different friends. In big ways and little ways, even close sisters don't have the same experiences.

So, if no two people exactly share life's experiences, and if their ideas and beliefs come from their individual, unique, experiences, how could they possible think alike? The short answer is they can't and they don't. Of course, the more similarity there is in their experience, the more similarity there is in their ideas. People of the same generation or gender or culture or even neighborhood often share more than those who are different, but no one's an exact copy of anyone else in experience, or in thought rising from that experience.

This is what happened with my piano students. Although we shared many experiences, such as language and interest in music, we differed in the simple fact that my experience included looking at a clock that wasn't working properly and theirs included looking at a clock that was. Now, I have to follow M. Scott Peck's advice and get reconciled—apologize and explain what went wrong so there's no longer any misunderstanding. The differences in our experience led to a potential difference in opinion, a conflict, which is normal, natural, and inevitable.

These differences are a good thing, because they make you unique and your potential contributions to the world incredibly special. It's also a sad thing, because it's what causes much of the loneliness of the human condition. We're born alone, we die alone, and in between we experience love and laughter and suffering and learning alone, despite the many people that may surround us. We are responsible for what we do with the gifts we've been given, and we are responsible for our strength, weakness, success, and failure in a very personal and individual way, even though we'd often like to share the credit or the blame. The thoughts we have, those incredibly individual and unique ideas, trigger our emotions and our actions, which in turn trigger real results in the world.

There are a couple of big lessons here. One is to look closely at our thoughts, since they will lead to our actions. We need to educate ourselves with the very best information available, test our thoughts against reality frequently, challenge those thoughts that are negative or too self-serving, and compare our thoughts with those of others whom we respect.

The second lesson is in how we do that comparison. Since we know that differences will always be part of the interaction between people, we have to work to communicate clearly, and to listen closely, to minimize the problem. If I had simply said to my piano students who showed up unexpectedly, "Oh my goodness, my clock says it's only three o'clock—what time does yours say?", there would have been no problem. Now, since I didn't do that, I am a bit embarrassed to have to admit how long it took me to figure out what went wrong. And, since I think this lesson is a basic one we all need to know from a very early age—nobody thinks like you—I'm also a little embarrassed about how long it has taken me to discuss it with you.

Workbook Questions:

1. Have you ever assumed someone thought as you did, only to discover that they didn't? Was that a problem?
2. List five or six people and experiences in your life that have shaped your thinking in an important way.
3. Can you select influences on your future thinking? Would it work to carefully select your friends, your reading material, your music, your activities? Would that make a difference?

Persistence

- Learn the power of sticking to a task
- Techniques for overcoming discouragement
- Small steps, taken every day, are the path of progress

Have you heard of the actor and director, Woody Allen? He once said that most of success is just showing up. Others, including me, would add that you have to show up again and again and again.

Many times, when I would give a speech to an organization, they would give me, in addition to the paycheck, a little gift. Most of those gifts found their way eventually into storage, but there's one that I still keep on a file cabinet in the office today, where I can see it when I need it. It's a little plaque that talks about persistence, and its title is *Press On*. It says, "Nothing in the world can take the place of persistence. Talent will not; nothing is more common than unsuccessful people with talent. Genius will not; unrewarded genius is almost a proverb. Education will not; the world is full of educated derelicts. Persistence and determination alone are omnipotent". That last word means all-powerful, and it's only a tiny bit of an exaggeration. Persistence, good old stick-to-it-iveness, is one of the most powerful tools you can have to achieve your goals and make a difference in this world.

Mr. Macy went bankrupt several times over before he successfully founded Macy's; Babe Ruth struck out a whole bunch of times, but he kept swinging, and he's remembered for his home runs. The author of a writing book I'm studying says she sent a manuscript in 17 times before it was published, and I know there are many writers who can tell of still more frustrating numbers of submissions. Even in the Bible, King Solomon is worn down by a petitioner's persistence, and gave her what she wanted, and Jesus himself granted the wish of a woman who kept at him. When he told her to go away, that the food (his words and his healing power) was for "the family", she reminded him that even the dogs get to have the scraps. (Matt. 15:22-28)

Persistence is such a lowly talent, so unglamorous, that it is often overlooked. It seems stubborn, even foolish, but it's powerful. The best example I know of from the natural world is water. Put your hand into a bucket of water; there's no resistance, it's yielding, almost soft. But think of the canyons worn by water working its steady, slow way down through the rock; think of the roads torn apart by water freezing and thawing. As gentle as it seems, water in its persistence is incredibly powerful.

There are many, many famous people who talk about the power of persistence in their lives. One of the most incredible is Thomas Alva Edison, whose inventions include the telephone, telegraph, electric lights, and many other things. He had a great deal to say about the significance of persistence. He is famous for the line, "Genius is one percent inspiration and ninety-nine percent perspiration", but he also said, "Many of life's failures are people who did not realize how close they were to success when they gave up." I also remember hearing that he said to one critic, "I now know ninety-nine ways not to invent a light bulb!" That's persistence!

When you're trying out for a role in a play, or a place on a team, for college entry, or for a job that you really want, persistence will be absolutely essential. There's a great deal of competition, and it's tempting to give up when your first choice says "no". But don't give up; keep trying and you will succeed. It's easy to get discouraged, and discouragement is the enemy of persistence. If you let that take over, the difficulties and obstacles in your path will seem too much for you. Just persevere, and be patient. With constant effort, at least a little every day, those roadblocks will magically disappear. It takes effort, and constant effort, to get where you want to go, but it's the only way. The old Irish saying has it, "Nodding the head does not row the boat". Grab those oars and keep rowing!

There will be some times when you have to be persistent in very tough circumstances. When your Dad faced the struggles of trying to keep up with kids, a demanding job, and full-time school all at once, I shared with him that every day in graduate school when I thought I was too tired to keep a schedule like that, I told myself, "You can do anything for a little while". It's true, too. I found out, and he's finding out, that you can summon almost superhuman endurance if you know that it's just for a short time.

One final story about persistence. When we came back to the US from Ethiopia, I applied for a job in the Foreign Service, took a test, and was called to Chicago for an interview. There was something not quite right about that interview—the two men asking the questions didn't seem to like any of my answers, and they actually argued about some of them, and laughed at others. I had a political science degree then, and was just back from working overseas, so I was sure that at least some of my answers were good. Later on, I found out that there were no women at all hired to be Foreign Service Officers during a 10-year period that included my interview, and the government's radio station, Voice of America, didn't hire any women then, either. The other qualified candidates and their lawyers began a lawsuit which took 25 years to finally be settled. But when it was, it was the largest discrimination settlement ever against the State Department. For twenty-five years, they persisted, and finally there were serious and much-needed changes made in the hiring process to be fairer to all candidates, and substantial back pay awards to all those who had been discriminated against. Both things were worth waiting for!

Many good things are well worth waiting, and working, for, no matter how long it takes. When you hit a wall, take heart, and ask yourself how to go over, around, or under it. And as Winston Churchill said during the Second World War, "Never, never, never, never give up."

Workbook Questions:

1. Why do you think some people give up easily? Are you one of them?
2. Can you think of an example from your own life of determination and persistence that led to success? What kept you going?
3. How do you know when to evaluate your strategy, make needed adjustments, and then keep trying, rather than just trying the same thing over and over?

Discipline

- Discipline is not about punishing others or being punished by others
- Choice leads to contentment, and discipline is the path between them
- Discipline might be about not doing something, or about doing something well
- The rewards of this dedication far outweigh the effort
- Motivating yourself to be disciplined is easier once this fulfillment pattern is clear

When you hear the word discipline, what do you think of—being sent to your room? Not having dessert? People who've had intelligent and loving parents, probably don't think of being hit or beaten, which is what quite a few less lucky people would say that word is all about. But still, I'll bet you don't think of anything very positive when you hear the word. I'm going to try to change your mind, because it's one of my favorite words, and you know I don't go around smacking people.

Lots of people have discipline and punishment confused. Punishment is a way of reacting to someone's behavior that you don't like—you try to stop the behavior you dislike and prevent it from happening again through the use of force. Unfortunately, punishment has lots of side effects that make it unlikely to work as a good way of shaping and controlling behavior. Let me explain. Pretend you're in school or college, and you forgot to do your math homework, and your teacher punished you by yelling at you and embarrassing you in front of everyone. Now, are you going to be eager to go to math class the next day? A child in that situation would probably try to convince his or her mom they have a stomachache so they can stay home and avoid the whole painful situation. So, if the teacher's job is to teach, he or she just made it difficult to do that job, because the student is not going to show up in class to be taught. Punishment often causes avoidance, or running away from the painful situation. If the person being punished can't actually run away, they might just mentally get out of there, daydreaming or sketching pictures instead of being fully present to learn. They might also spread some nasty rumors about the teacher, because getting even is another side effect of punishment. To use another example, if you want a donkey to go forward and it doesn't want to, you might punish it by hitting it with a stick. Now, the donkey might go forward, but the donkeys I've seen might just as easily kick you—getting even. Even in the best of circumstances, punishment stops working when the person doing the punishing goes away—the behavior is not really learned, or owned, it's just done to stop the punishment. So, that donkey will stop going in the direction you wanted once you turn your attention to something else—it isn't really trained, it's just trying to get away from the stick.

Discipline is something else, and something altogether better. The unabridged dictionary on the hall table says that discipline is training to act in accordance with rules, and that it's activity, exercise, or a regimen that develops or improves a skill. It also shows the close connection between the word discipline and the word disciple, which gives you a clue about why I like the word so much. For me, it's about choosing a path, and choosing to follow that path day after day, even when it's not easy. It's about a way of living that requires your attention, effort, concentration, and dedication.

In order to give something you've chosen all that attention, effort, and so on, you have to believe that it's the best way of living. Here's where you really separate yourself from the crowd. People who think the best part of life is retirement, and the best part of the year is vacation, and the best part of the week is the weekend, and the best part of the day is when school or work is over, don't believe in this kind of discipline. They study and work so they can stop studying and working. People who are disciplined study and work at their chosen field so they can live fulfilling lives, which probably will involve a lot more studying and working. That's quite a difference.

Discipline works for big things and little things, and it's available to you at any time at all. When you wanted to learn how to ice skate, how did you do it? Did you start out being really good at it? Did you have to take it step-by step, and endure some nasty falls? Did you have to try it more than once? That took some discipline. Now, just imagine the discipline it takes for working students who are parents to get their education completed. Like my son Michael, they've had to work and take classes and do homework, and cook and help take care of the family, and go without very much sleep for many years. Do you think there have been times when the temptation was strong to do something else besides study, and they studied anyway? That's discipline. They have to believe that the result will be worth all the sacrifice of working that hard for that long.

Now, think about what it is that makes them go through all that. Did someone else force them? Would they have been punished if they stopped part way through college? No, this is a drive and a discipline that's built into people like this, something that's a part of their very being. It comes from a decision that the kind of life they wanted for themselves and for their families required this effort, and they stick with it despite the fact that there are some very difficult times.

Next, think about a person you know who holds strong religious beliefs, and has to live in a certain way because of that. Are they being forced to give up certain pleasures that others enjoy? Is it a kind of punishment, after all? Or is this a part of their belief structure, something makes their life worthwhile and uniquely theirs?

The point is that effective discipline is chosen. We choose to live a certain way, work very hard for a certain goal, avoid some things and seek others, because of what we know and what we believe about the good and fulfilling life. For me, trying to live in a disciplined way brings a great deal of contentment along with some real progress towards my goals. Practicing piano for an hour every day, for example, means that I can teach some wonderful students, and that when the church needs someone to play, I can step in and do that job easily. Reading a chapter of the Bible every day keeps my heart full of wonder and gratitude. Swimming and walking every day means that my body stays healthy, and because Captain Bob walks with me, we have a quiet time to talk about things every morning and evening. And the dogs love the exercise, too. Discipline doesn't have to be nasty or exhausting. It can also be fun, and very, very rewarding.

Workbook Questions:

1. What's the first thing you've always thought of when you hear the word "discipline"? What new thoughts do you have now about its meaning?
2. What single goal in your life have you given the most concentrated effort to? Was the process worth it, and how so?
3. What one change would you like to make in your life, but have been afraid that it would be too difficult? Can you see any way to begin to make that change now?
4. What have you consciously chosen not to do, to avoid, in your life? Why? Are you satisfied with this choice?
5. If you had to explain how discipline leads to contentment, what would you say?

Good Enough For Who It's For

- Poor service is a form of contempt
- The value of servant leadership
- The truth of the old motto, "If it's worth doing, it's worth doing well"

Back in the 1960s, we were living in Boulder, Colorado and going to graduate school at the University there. It was a beautiful place, we were very young, and there was lots to see and do and learn. Eileen was a baby, and we lived in a pretty little 4 room rented house. Most of the time I loved it there. It was the first time I had been a "grown-up" married woman living in a separate house with a husband and baby, working and going to school.

One day the landlord decided to paint the kitchen, which certainly needed it. We had put in bookshelves all along one wall, and it looked pretty messy, with all those book cover colors and a wall of peeling paint. I was busy with the baby while he worked, and saw after awhile that he was cleaning up to go, but a lower part of the wall was still unpainted. I pointed it out to him, and he laughed and said "It's good enough for who it's for!" Perhaps he meant to be funny, or maybe he had run out of paint, or maybe he was just being lazy, but why did he have to insult us that way? You know it made an impact, and not a good one, since I can remember it clearly these many years afterwards.

Later in life, I heard that same misplaced joking, that same disrespect, in the phrase "Good enough for government work!" I don't believe it fits there, either. This is about standards, of believing in what you're doing, that it deserves your time and attention, and that you will give it your best shot. It's also about respect and service.

I'm not saying you need to make a major project out of everything you do for someone else. Rather, I'm saying that to give more than is expected, not less, is to show respect for the other person. It demonstrates a service attitude. In business now, it's fashionable among some highly educated and thoughtful people to talk about, and to try to live, the idea of servant leadership. Of course the idea is much older than this current trend. Jesus said "Whosoever would be chiefest, shall be servant of all"(Mark 10:44). I think it's interesting to remember when he said that, his disciples were quarreling over who would be greatest in the coming kingdom. So maybe when we are competing with another person, that's when we should think about serving them instead.

My sister sent me an interesting email attachment that gave me some insight about this. It seems that a plainly dressed couple called unexpectedly on Harvard University's President, who kept them waiting most of the day. When he finally stepped out to see what they wanted and send them away, they said they wanted to donate a memorial to their son, a Harvard graduate who had died the last year. He ridiculed them, telling them he was sure they had no idea what a memorial building would cost. So, they left and Mr. and Mrs. Leland Stanford went to Palo Alto, California and established Stanford University there in memory of their son. The Harvard President who had treated them so disrespectfully lost the opportunity to strengthen his school, and instead wound up with serious competition for the best minds in the country. He made a snap judgment about his rude treatment being "good enough for who it's for", and he was wrong.

That's no surprise. Such a judgment is usually wrong. When I started giving training seminars, one of my first client companies was a corporate ranch in central California. I was training supervisors, and the last one into the room came straight from his tractor, dirty, with broken teeth and filthy boots, which he stuck out and crossed right in front of me. I'm glad I held back on my opinion, though, because soon he grinned and said "I've been waiting for a chance like this all my life!"

Those words are music to any teacher's ears, and he swiftly became a favorite student. "Good enough for who it's for" should always be, and only be, your very best.

Workbook Questions:

1. Have you ever been tempted to cut corners on the quality of a project you're doing? What was the result? How did you feel about that?
2. Some very low-prioritiy jobs don't have to be done to the highest standards, but service is never a low-priority job. Do you agree or disagree?
3. Does giving more than is expected set you apart in a good way, or does it make you seem foolish, an "easy mark"?

Renaissance People

- Everyone has multifaceted capabilities
- Interests change throughout the lifespan
- Avoid the trap of becoming one of the "living dead"

There's a lovely woman I know, the mother of two of my piano students and a pilot for United Airlines, who was teasing me the other day. She'd been asking about the diplomas in my office, and the experiences I have had. When we talked about my having trained in a small plane, the Piper Tomahawk, she snapped at me, "You've done that too?" She wasn't really angry, just frustrated that it appeared as if I'd had lots of chances to do different things, and maybe she felt regret at not having tried some things. I get that reaction sometimes, and I always tell people that I believe we're all Renaissance People inside, and we need to express that in our lives. You probably already know that during the Renaissance, there was a widespread revival of the arts and learning in Europe. Some people, like Leonardo daVinci, seemed to be able to do many different things extremely well. He was renowned as a scientist, engineer, painter, sculptor, musician, and mathematician. In contrast, since at least the 19th century, people generally do one thing pretty well, and maybe several other things nearly as well, but their reputation rests on the thing they have done best, or longest. Now, I don't think it's the people and their innate talents that have changed. I think it is society's expectations that have changed, and it's our loss. Some say that the world of work has gotten more difficult, and standards are so high now that we have to dedicate ourselves to training long and hard in order to be really good at anything. I disagree, for I can't see anything low about daVinci's standards, or Michelangelo's. Granted, we don't have lots of staff around to pick up after us, and we do generate more laundry and dishes to clean by our lifestyle, but we have appliances to help with all that.

I'll bet that sometimes you spend a lot of time thinking about what you want to do when you're grown. Notice I said what you want to *do*; not what you want to *be*; you already are somebody. What you want to do is a big question, but not a life-or-death one. You have interests and abilities you know about already; let them guide you in the beginning. You can start in one direction then change and go another direction. It's not a crime, and it might even be interesting. Your Aunt Heather used to joke that she was on the 7-year college plan, because she changed her mind about what she wanted to study so often. Now, she's very happy and very capable as a nurse. She's also a very good cook and an excellent mom, and has a lively interest in decorating. Perhaps some day she will choose to pursue one of those other interests in a different kind of job. Aunt Eileen is a terrific lawyer, and she's also got a great business sense; I wouldn't be surprised if she is a success in her own company. Your Dad was a marvelous chef before he even started studying as an engineer. Uncle Brian thinks he wants to work in construction, but he's also a very good listener for his friends who are troubled, so he would make a good counselor, and he has a very kind heart when it comes to animals, so he'd be a good vet.

The point is, everyone, not just people in our family, has multiple talents and interests. We might find ourselves working in different careers over the years to express those interests, or we might develop some of them as hobbies, or maybe they are the center of our retirement plan—at last, time to do something about that interest! We need to be clear-headed about saving for retirement so we aren't too dependent on any one career's pension plan, and there are some other adjustments we need to make as well, but it's entirely possible to shape your life around all your talents and interests, rather than just one. That's what Renaissance People are—well-rounded, fully developed, full of life and plans and goals and the excitement of waking up each day wondering who we're becoming today! What a contrast to the "living dead"—people who stopped reading and looking and learning when they left school, and spend their work lives repeating the first year forty times, and their leisure lives passively watching other people act out imitation lives on TV.

Each morning arrives full of possibility, full of promise and demand. You'll need all your equipment in working order to respond. Sometimes you'll need one talent, and sometimes, another. From one Renaissance person to another, I hope you'll keep all your talents polished, your tools sharpened and ready, and take on each day with all your vigor from the time you first open your eyes, to the time you can't keep them open any longer!

Workbook Questions:

1. List at least three different interests you have that might turn into careers. How can you keep all of them alive?
2. Track the amount of time you devote to passive things like watching TV. Can you carve out some of this time for studying a new field of interest?
3. What's keeping you from trying to learn about an interest of yours? Whose judgment do you fear? What benefits might you gain?

On Being American

- The essence of responsible freedom
- Your involvement is crucial
- Ambivalence doesn't justify withdrawal from the debate

Sometimes when we're at a 4th of July celebration, or a parade, I cry a little, often a lot, when the flags go by. Those tears are three-quarters pride and gratitude, and one-quarter frustration. I've probably talked more about the frustration part, and so I wanted a chance to talk about it all just a little bit, to set the record straight about how it's possible both to love your country very much, to be passionately proud and grateful about it, and at the same time, to be so angry with some of its leaders that you could spit nickels.

During the time that we lived in Ethiopia, where your Dad was born, there was a revolution. The emperor, Haile Selassie, was imprisoned and killed. A military group took over, and the transition from one government to the other was pretty rough. Scary things happened, and security was tight. One example of that was the Post Office. To get our mail, I had to be searched first, and then could go in and get the mail, which had already been opened, read, and valuables removed. One day, the woman in front of me in line objected to the search, and spoke sharply to the soldier. To show her who was in charge, he hit her in the face with his rifle butt. Believe me, I didn't question him after that! Now, in the US, people sometimes complain about the Post Office, saying the mail is slow, or things get lost now and then, or the price of stamps keeps going up. But, you know, my US mailman never hit me in the face with his rifle butt. And my mail is never opened and important things aren't taken out of the envelope before I can get them.

Years later, two Russian friends I had met while working in Siberia came to stay with us in Stockton so we could work together. I remember their amazement at our wonderful roads in California, even away from the cities, and at how often people walking down the street would smile at them for no reason. Yes, the basics and much, much more are firmly in place in America; the Post Office works, the roads are good, and people smile because they can, living in such a land of beauty, bounty, and opportunity.

And there's a lot to smile about, indeed, lucky souls that we are to have been born in a place where people from all over the world beat down the doors to get in, a place where the ideas of freedom and human rights have come out to play, a place with comfort levels even Cleopatra never could have imagined. We can all run for office, we can all vote, we can make our voices heard on the local, state, and national levels, we can join groups that campaign for or against various policies. Education is free, and so is assembly—we can stand together with like-minded people to urge changes that improve lives for many. The people who sacrificed their wealth and their lives to establish this country, and the people who fought to protect it, should rightly be honored by us all. On the other hand, those who are too lazy to vote and too busy watching TV and drinking beer to pay tribute to freedom's defenders on national holidays are a sorry lot indeed.

And yet, and yet, there is so much more that our nation could be and do. We have fallen far short of the standards set by the country's founders. Greed rules in most political centers. Special interests buy the votes they want and the rest of us have to live with policies that benefit them, not us. Lies are told, truths withheld, shameful acts covered up, and corruption hides behind closed doors, as surely as in any third-world tyranny. But in the US, the media sometimes seeks the truth, at least as much as they seek corporate sponsors. And in every era, a few brave individuals have had the courage to take unpopular public stands in the name of conscience. We can change our minds, and our leaders, quite often to make the needed course corrections. That opportunity to change is what public debates and elections are all about.

You'll hear, in addition to the names of the most prominent political parties, the Republicans and the Democrats, the words liberal and conservative. Those are interesting words, and they offer two viewpoints about how problems are best solved and the country best governed. I think that Conservatives in general believe in individual responsibility, and that if government gets out of the way, people will solve their own problems, and voluntarily contribute to the public good. And it seems that Liberals, on the other hand, believe in general that the playing field is not level, and that some people need a little boost from the government in order to get to where they can begin to solve their own problems, and they don't trust individual charity to take care of all public problems. That's a shorthand version, but it gives you an idea of the terms of the debate. Many quote Winston Churchill on this subject: "Any man who is under 30 and is not a liberal has no heart, and any man who is over 30 and is not a conservative, has no brain." This famous statement refers to how much people stand to gain and lose by their political choices, for older people usually have more property, so are more interested in protecting it through conservative political choices.

A very recent finding has it that there is a genetic component in these political choices, in addition to early family influence. If this is so, it's even more important to avoid blaming people who think differently from you. Whichever of these ideas makes the most sense to you now, keep thinking about them, and keep observing people you know and listening to their arguments. An active involvement in this debate is, I believe, a responsibility of anyone lucky enough to live where such debates are possible.

So, to be an American, responsibly free, means to be part of the discussion. It also means to take action in your community, whether that's cleaning up graffiti, painting houses for seniors who can't paint their own any longer, serving as a volunteer for a campaign, or playing an instrument in a patriotic parade. I hope you will be part of inspiring your generation to make America all that it could, and should, be.

When I was doing some research on optimism, I found that kids born in America weren't as optimistic as kids who had come into the country as immigrants, or whose parents were immigrants. They didn't have as much hope for the future, and I found that sad. Restoring that optimism, inspiration, and gratitude is a huge job, and a hugely important one.

Workbook Questions:

1. For you, what is the best part of being an American? The worst part?
2. Do you feel it is important to be involved in your community? Do your friends agree?
3. What can you personally do to bee sure many viewpoints are represented in discussion of political and community issues?

Chapter 5

Meditations and Musings on the Meaning of It All

Tolerance

- Learn to expand your range of comfort with differences
- Law guards our behavior; only we can guard our thoughts
- Achieving tolerance is the work of a lifetime

I'd like you to think for a moment about a few people you know, like and understand. How different are they from you? How different from each other? Give this some real thought, for it's important to know your range of comfort, and to keep stretching it until you can truly embrace the world. The name for this acceptance is tolerance, a word I didn't much like until recently, despite my training in cross-cultural psychology. I thought it too lukewarm a word, too intellectual, rather than heartfelt, but now I've become more, shall we say, tolerant, of it.

Voltaire defined tolerance as the first law of nature, and saw it as the consequence of humanity. We are all formed of frailty and error; he said, let us pardon reciprocally each other's folly. Others have remarked how much we already have fulfilled the commandment to love our neighbors as ourselves, for if we don't love ourselves, we tend to be pretty hard on our neighbors as well, and if we've learned to love ourselves, we extend that caring to others. In the best of circumstances, that is the case, but those circumstances are far from universal, and intolerance seems to have a pretty strong grip on much of the world. Sadly, most of the world's wars have their root cause in intolerance, as does an inexcusably sizeable amount of common, everyday rudeness and outright mistreatment of one another.

The United States, as you know, was founded on tolerance, particularly on religious tolerance. Many of those who migrated to the US from Europe were fleeing religious persecution, and so they were at pains to create a nation where no one religion could become the "official" religion, excluding others. They were after freedom of religion, not freedom from religion, but that point seems to have been somewhat overlooked of late. The concept of tolerance was greatly extended in 1964 with the passage of the Civil Rights Act, which provided that employers were not to discriminate in hiring, work conditions, promotion, or discipline on the basis of race, religion, national origin, or sex. In 1967, discrimination in the workplace on the basis of age was prohibited by law. And later still, the American Disabilities Act extended such protections to those with disabilities. Very many lawsuits and very, very many training seminars later, improvements in access and in the fairness of work conditions are so widespread as to be very encouraging, even if the playing field still remains somewhat uneven.

The law, of course, speaks to our behavior, and limits it in ways that the nation has determined will best serve the greater good. We can't drive through red lights, we can't simply take what we want from a window display, we can't kill people we're angry with. If everyone behaved on whim alone, chaos would reign. The law, though, says nothing at all, nor can it, about our thoughts, and that is why the remnants of intolerance are rooted so deeply and spring up in such widespread places. And that is where the work of tolerance remains to be done. Forcing people who don't understand or accept each other to work together without overt conflict is only a very small first step. It's far more important that all involved learn why valuing, actually appreciating, differences is both healthy and productive. Someone from a different background thinks differently than you do, and if you haven't been able to figure out the answer to a puzzle, that difference may provide just the needed resource. In the business world, those companies that have aggressively promoted the valuing of diversity have been proven right, where it counts in that world, at the bottom line of profitability.

But in our private lives, we're not so concerned with profit, we want comfort, and diversity certainly challenges that. The roots of our discomfort go very deep into our childhood, when caregivers told us in what ways we and our family were special, implying that outsiders were not as special. We need to learn how to give children the first part of that message, and omit the second, untrue, harmful, part. It's important to grow beyond this small-mindedness if we are truly to become global citizens. One of the things I especially loved about Fresno, and later, Stockton, was exactly the diversity—there were so many wonderful foods to try, and so many delightful festivals to celebrate, and so many kinds of music to hear and enjoy! Those are great places to learn to appreciate the specialness of others, and to practice global citizenship.

Yet another place where intolerance still holds sway in America is, sadly, is in some of its churches. There is a great deal of mystery, love, and compassion in the Lord, but we don't always hear that; instead we hear the language of intolerance. God calls whom He will, the Spirit moveth where It will, and this is not our business, but His. We are called to live aright, to love our neighbors, to testify to the truth as we understand it, and to search for the path of obedience to God's will. We do not have God in our pocket; instead we can only pray to be in His. Part of loving our neighbor, I believe, is to allow them to tell the truth as they understand it, and to let them know where we are in agreement and where not, and even to pray for enlightenment. The rest is God's work.

I said, in beginning to write to you about this, that I thought the word tolerance too lukewarm to love. I wanted to rush past it into full-fledged cherishing of the different, wondrous, other. Now I realize that there are some of the different ones that I don't find wondrous at all, but rather poor in the gifts of character, too small-minded, too cruel, too heartbreakingly closed to love. And so it will take me a lifetime to fully achieve tolerance. Mother Teresa got way beyond tolerance, to love the unlovable, but then, she's a candidate for sainthood, and I'm not. And I'm learning to tolerate myself as I struggle with this, too. May these thoughts make your journey to loving others less of a struggle.

Workbook Questions:

1. Think about your range of comfort—who are the oldest and youngest people you are comfortable with? The races, religions, educational levels you interact with easily. Can you work to expand this a little at a time?
2. Where in your community can you find a way to interact with those different from you?
3. Why is valuing others who are different both healthy and profitable?

Family

- There is a forever quality to family
- Structural changes need not dilute the functionality of family
- How to strengthen family interaction to best teach values and civic responsibility

There's a black wood sculpture from Kenya in the living room. It's softly burnished, about a foot and a half tall, a few inches in diameter. There are a number of people arranged around the form, standing on each other's shoulders, from the bottom to the top, on all sides. An African man told me that this represents a village, with each generation standing on the shoulders of the prior generation as it reaches upward in its quest for life. I like to think of it as a family, each age group holding up the next and helping it. There's another wood sculpture in the room, one I've called "Still together after all these years." It represents to me a family group as well, with some leaning on others, the big ones holding on to the little ones, the weak supported by the strong, and all tilted just a little inward, toward each other, to comfort and to speak encouragement in each other's ears.

Family is something of an endangered species in the US, with high divorce rates and lots of people moving away from their homes as soon as they can. Because we haven't quite lost the whole idea yet, it's worth remembering what the family ideal is for, and thinking how to restore it so it works in a new era. In some ways, family is forever. One side of my family can be traced to the Mayflower, which counted for something where we lived. Even if the whole bunch had been horse thieves, it's still important to know what you can of your genetic background, for health reasons, and to help explain character a little. Because some of my kids are adopted, I tried to learn what I could of their genetic background for them. Family certainly doesn't have to be blood ties, and usually half of it is marriage ties instead. And then there are the close friends of parents, surrogate aunts and uncles, that so enrich everyone's lives. Part of what makes family special is this forever quality, the knowing that whatever you do, wherever you go, you'll still be daughter to these two, granddaughter and cousin and niece to these others, and that will never change. Later, you'll add the titles of wife, mom, aunt, and still later, grandmother, and all of these roles are good, right, and meaningful. At different times in your lives, when you have different needs and interests, some of these roles will be more powerful than others, but they'll all be there, waiting their turn in the cycle of life.

I'm reading a biography now called *Change me into Zeus's Daughter*, by Barbara Robinette Moss. It's the hard story of her impoverished childhood in the rural South, a life of want, malnutrition, violence, alcoholism, and the cruel taunting of schoolmates. But it's also a beautiful story of family love, brave and protective older brothers, a caring aunt, a fragile mother who did the best she could, and small sustaining acts of kindness from neighbors and strangers. The laughter and caring shown among all the children in these daunting circumstances illustrates the tensile strength of family; its ability to provide nurturing for the spirit even in the most tragic circumstances. Because there are few secrets here, and nowhere to hide, the acceptance is real.

One of the things that's changing so rapidly as to threaten family structure is the role of each person. Traditionally, father earned, mother kept the home, and children did as they were told, growing into responsibility and maturity at a steady pace. Grandparents may have lived in the home, or nearby, and the occasional out of work uncle or the aunt needing refuge with her baby were taken in without question or reluctance. I don't know if it ever actually happened just that way, but that was the model. Economic changes have made it necessary for both parents to work if they can find work, and children often go far away for schooling and to start their own families. In times of recession, however, the extended family, grandparents, aunts and uncles, still come home to roost. So who earns, who cares for the house, who cooks and shops, who drives to all the after school activities, who meets with the teacher? In many cases, the answer is, whoever is available. In a single-parent home, or a home with two adult partners, these decisions have to be made with an eye both to what's possible, and what's best for the young. That certainly doesn't make people less male or female, just more flexible. We are in the process, as a culture, of redesigning the family structure, and each person's part in it, and it's terribly important that we don't lose the good things in the process. The safety, security, acceptance, and nurturing that each person, and each child, especially, has the right to expect in the arms of the family is a cultural treasure well worth protecting.

Families are the places where we are formed, where we learn how to act in the world. If we are taught to limit our desires out of consideration for others, we become law-abiding. If we learn to do chores as a natural part of living, we learn to care for our planet as well. We learn how to act when health fails, what to do with both success and failure, and what's expected of us with regard to our neighbors. There is no greater service any parents can give to their nation than to raise children who question considerately, act intelligently, temper their wants out of regard for other's needs, and abide by rules, knowing that they can come together to change them when necessary. We used to have family meetings quite frequently, and everyone had a say, although the parents reserved the right to veto unaffordable or illegal actions. I hope you've continued that tradition, and that you will bring to the next generation of family mutual respect, sound guidance, and a great, great deal of love and patience.

Workbook Questions:

1. Can values be taught in only one form of the family?
2. Think of the most cohesive, healthy family you know. How are the necessary roles and tasks organized?
3. What are the options for someone whose family is less than nurturing?

Angels

- Seeing is truly believing
- Angels teach us to move forward through fear
- Encouragement and comfort are gifts angels bring

In medieval Europe, serious people used to debate how many angels could dance on the head of a pin! That seems absurd to us now, but we still don't understand very much about the subject. The Bible is full of angel stories, and some of the most wonderful hymns have lines like "I know that there are angels all around". But popular culture has way too many cutesy plastic, ceramic, and paper angels for many people to take them seriously, and believing in angels seems for lots of bright people to be just a charming, but old-fashioned and primitive, superstition.

I never thought much at all about angels growing up, or even during most of my adult life. Then I saw one and it changed everything. Now, I don't just *believe* in angels, I *know* there are angels. That's different, sort of like doubting Thomas having to put his hand in the wound to be sure it was Jesus talking to him. I had always hoped there were angels, powerful and merciful beings who would rescue and sustain us in troubled times, but I didn't know for sure. There had been hints, though. One time when I was out walking and arguing terribly with my husband, I felt nothing but the deepest despair, and threw myself down in a grassy area to weep. Out of nowhere, a beautiful calico cat raced over and began to wind around my feet, purring and comforting me. Although I walked there many other times, I never saw the cat again. After that, I wondered if angels might come in the form of beautiful, loving animals.

But the time I stopped wondering and knew for sure, I wasn't unhappy at all. In fact, it was one of the loveliest vacations of my life. Alan and I were in Brianhead, Utah, a place surrounded by some of the finest scenery on earth. We were driving down the mountain, headed for a hike in Zion National Park, when I saw something odd in the woods by the road. There was a person standing just a few yards from the road, in the trees, but the scene didn't look quite right. Have you ever seen one of those name cards they paste in books—they're called bookplates? Well, many of them are woodcuts and look very medieval. That's how this person looked—tall, strong, in a flowing robe, and holding a long staff in his hand. Just behind him, being held back by the staff, were many, many serpents and snakes—monsters so ugly they could not possibly be real. And the whole scene was more in black and white than in color, which made it look even more medieval. It was only in my awareness for a second or two, and we traveled on. After a dazed few minutes, I said to Alan, "You'll never believe what I just saw!", and I told him about the figure and the snakes. Then, I said, "It's almost as if there are terrible things coming our way, but we're being protected, and given this perfect time together first, before the troubles come." I was almost right—soon after that he was dead, and I experienced the worst harassment and persecution I'd ever known. That angel had given us a golden moment, and fair warning of what was to come.

There was another gift as well, and that was strengthened faith. When the troubles came, I knew for sure that there were protecting angels, and that even though I did not understand why horrible things were happening, God did, and this too would pass. At Alan's funeral I asked the pastor to speak from Job, who, in his own time of terrible grief was able to say, "The Lord giveth and the Lord taketh away; blessed be the name of the Lord." (Job 1:21)

Whenever an angel greets a person in the Bible, the first words out of the angel's mouth are almost always, "Fear not." It's never, "Hello, I'm going to explain some things to you", and it's not "What can I do for you?" either. Just, "Fear not." I find that very interesting. Think about the things you're afraid of. What would life be like if you could just get past that fear? It seems that when we get instructions, that's what we're told—go on through the fear and get it done, whatever we're supposed to do.

The angel I saw said nothing, just stood there protecting us for a time. Years later, when I thought about it, I remembered an earthly version of that experience long ago while camping at a Rift Valley lake in Ethiopia. There was a man named, improbably, Oopsie, who stood all night in his robe, holding a spear, alongside the car I was sleeping in. He was my protector for the night. I have to admit that I didn't sleep much, and did giggle quite a bit about the protector I saw as delightful but unnecessary. I didn't sense any danger, after all.

But the angel who came to warn and protect left a much more powerful and lasting impression, together with the gift of certainty about God's care and the gift of at least a little courage to press on. Did you know that your Dad's name, Michael, is after a mighty angel? I trust that you will find your own protectors when you need them and you're ready to see them, and those angels will be even stronger and more dedicated to you than your Dad is.

Workbook Questions:

1. What could you accomplish if only you could move past your fears?
2. Have you, or someone close to you, ever had an experience with an angel? What changed as a result of that?
3. Why do you think TV programs and books about angels have such a large following?

Travel

- Travel challenges and changes us
- We can find differences at home and similarities abroad, as readily as the opposite
- Opportunities for travel come in many ways—say yes!

Heather called today and said that she'd like to bring little Carson to visit us in Mexico soon. She didn't say it was because he misses his grandma. She said she wanted to bring him because he doesn't have any stamps on his passport yet. I laughed with recognition and delight—she certainly has the family travel bug, and she intends to pass it on!

There was a time when I collected "conveyances", ways of getting around—I wanted to ride on every kind of transportation there was, just to say that I'd done it. Before I got tired of the game, I had a list with several different sizes of cars, trucks, planes, and boats, as well as trains, chairlifts, trams, bikes, motorcycles, skis, horses, even a camel.

It got me to wondering why we travel, despite the inconveniences, and why it's so important to share these experiences with our children. You two have been to Oregon, California, Hawaii and Mexico, and maybe we'll all make it to Paris soon. You've been studying your French, and I've been watching for sale prices on European travel on my favorite computer sites. Why, if it's so expensive, and so much work, do we want to go?

I hope it's because we recognize that our way of doing things, of understanding things, is very limited, and only one of many possible ways. Travel shows us some of those other ways, and we get to consider the pros and cons of each perspective. Sometimes the comparisons are really fun and affirming, letting us feel, for awhile, that we truly live in a small world.

One time in Siberia, I was on a Navy boat refurbished for tourists on Lake Baikal, and the local woman sitting next to me tugged at my white pants, and then at her white pants, and smiled. I saw she was finding ways we were alike, and I smiled and nodded. Next, she touched my hair, then hers, roughly the same shade, and again I smiled and nodded. Finally, she poked at the skin on my arm, a little pale in spite of sunburn, and she poked at hers, much ruddier, and sadly shook her head. I laughed at her exaggeration of our difference. Soon, we were in the galley, fixing lunch together for the others along on this short tour, and although the language barrier remained, I felt we were friends.

A few years earlier, I had been on a glass-bottom boat just off Acapulco when it stopped to pick up a couple dressed much more conservatively than the tourists. The woman's modest dress and head covering interested me, and I noted that she carried a Bible. Soon, she began to sing in the sweetest voice, and after a few notes, I realized it was a hymn I knew. I joined her on the chorus, harmonizing with her melody, and even though we were singing in different languages, our hearts carried the same message.

Both of those trips were relatively short, a week or two, and that's probably the way you'll travel most of the time. They were significantly different in one way, however, because I was a tourist in Mexico, but working in Russia. When you have an opportunity to work in another country, another culture, take it—nothing will ever look the same to you after that. That opportunity was very brief, but on other occasions, I've been able to work overseas for a year or more, and highly recommend the experience. It's one thing to be passing though, intent on extracting the most fun and knowledge from a few days. It's quite another thing to be living and working in another culture, making your way around the fresh food markets, auto repair shops, churches, bakeries and stores to find all the necessities of life. You have to struggle with the language, respect the calendar and customs, appreciate those who show you how or where, and stretch, stretch, stretch your worldview.

You'll have a chance in college to study abroad at least for a semester. You'll have opportunities like Peace Corps and study tours. Consider them carefully, and be brave—choose the ones that appeal to you, where you think you might make a difference, and you might become different. But above all, choose to go. Go for the shock of the different, for the peace of dropping out from the demands of your ordinary lives, the startle of discovering yourself through others' eyes, the amazing beauty of this incredible world. Go ride a camel for Grandma, and laugh at how terrible they smell, how mean they are, and how wonderful it is anyway!

Workbook Questions:

1. What is the place you've traveled to that was the most different from your home? Would you go again?
2. How do you change when you experience another culture?
3. Where in the world do you think your ideas would be most challenged? Would you consider going there?

Books

- Books are a window into the world experiences and souls of others
- Reading provides a contemplative respite in times of change
- Discussion of books provides a way to better understand others

The summer I turned 14, I spent on the dock at our family's Adirondack camp, reading Kipling and Poe, stories to fascinate, terrify, and above all, take me away for awhile from the confusing changes in my body and feelings. The year and a half we lived in Ethiopia, in addition to having a baby (your Dad, of course), and teaching art, I volunteered at the American Embassy Library, partly to have first choice of the most wonderful books, stories of familiar places, so reassuring during all the difficulties of that time and place. This last two years, since we've lived in Mexico, I've read nearly 150 books, on top of remodeling our house, writing, teaching piano, making friends, and learning how to get along most of the time in a very different culture. There's a theme here, isn't there? When things are crazy, new, frightening, or just too much, reading will give you a "time out", a chance to let everything sort itself out. After an hour, or a day, with a book, I find I'm readier to face the challenge and promise of my "real" life.

There's a bonus, too. Some of the best of these books I've read with others in book clubs, giving us all a chance to test ideas, sort out feelings, and get to know each other. Did you know your Grandfather Dell has been in the same book club almost 40 years? How nice to have those friendships, so stable over the changes of the years.

Your living room has lots of books; your aunts Eileen and Heather have good-sized bookcases in their living rooms, too. I'm so glad! It's probably a safe bet that you will have bookcases full of wonderful stuff wherever you make your homes, too. How are your favorite characters coming along with their series of "unfortunate events"? The last time I saw you both, your Dad had just bought another in that series for you. It's so wonderful to see you enjoy reading so much—what worlds it opens for you! You get to imagine life in other places, other times, and to try to put yourselves in the place of others, even when they are doing things you would never do. Reading has so many gifts, many of them you've already found, and others you'll discover throughout your lives.

Besides providing you with a safe haven in times of trouble or confusion, reading can instruct, enlarge, lead, inspire, get you thinking differently and more deeply. Very often it will change your life. When I was a child, one of my favorite stories had to do with a princess who adopted children from many countries. It was pretty insensitive, probably, even a bit racist, but it got me started on a path that led to lots of travel, and to my eventual interest and work in cross-cultural psychology. As a teen, I read Albert Schweitzer's biography, and became more committed to music, to faith, to travel, to kindness to animals. Already you both have read some books that might have planted seeds in your minds about possible interests and even careers, work that would be meaningful and fulfilling for you.

I'd very much like to help you build a library. We'll need to get biographies of people who have done wonderful things, overcome illness, poverty, and other obstacles, led lives of great value. We'll want to have some books that help explain the world—why things work and look the way they do, from computers to butterflies to baked Alaska. You may already know what fiction you want for now, and what books help you understand and apply the stories and parables of the Bible to everyday life. You might want some self-help books, especially those that help you understand the changes that go along with growing up. How about some simply beautiful books, filled with photographs of the stars, or drawings of flowers, or reproductions of the world's museum masterpieces? Or some books that are simply beautiful works of art themselves? Do you remember the old copy of Dicken's *The Christmas Carol* that's on our coffee table every Christmas? I love the gilt-edged pages, the suede cover, the fact that it was a gift from someone who stimulated my interest in the arts.

You see, once you get started, there's simply no end to it. And that's the point. Books are not about endings, about making things small, simple, and neat. Books are about enlarging, leading to the next thing, and the next after that . . . , and the next after that. What a marvelous, magical, mind-boggling trip it is, and you've already started!

Workbook Questions:

1. List your ten favorite books. Are any of them new friends? Do you think the list will change again soon?
2. What kinds of books are worth keeping? Why?
3. What do you learn about people when you discuss a book with them?

Music

- Music is about expressing the inexpressible
- The listener brings his or her meaning to the musical conversation
- Music is a cross-culturally understood language of all the deep emotions

Words about music fall so far short of the thing itself; I wish I could play this letter to you on the piano. You would come into the room, find a comfortable seat, sit back, relax, close your eyes, and wait for it to begin. Soon the low bass notes would strum a steady rhythm. A melody would join, softly, tenderly at first, gradually bringing in more and more voices until there's a celebratory choir whispering, then murmuring, then shouting. Then silence. Next, a low, sad bass tune tells of injustice and loss, and it's echoed by minor arpeggios in the treble, weeping and trembling. Then, a clear, strong lead voice takes over, reassuring, calling, insisting on courage, and you follow, wondering, and glad. The rhythm of life, the sounds of beasts and birds, elders and children, water and wind. You sigh, a tear forms, then a sweet smile, and you feel less alone.

In Robert Jourdain's beautiful book, *Music, The Brain, and Ecstasy*, he is at pains to point out that the meaning of music is not in the notes themselves, but in what they bring to consciousness in us. "When we bring our own life situations to music, we can make of music what we will . . . (it) idealizes emotions negative and positive . . . momentarily perfect(ing) our individual emotional lives . . . to make them beautiful . . . (B)y imparting pleasure even to negative emotions, music serves to justify sufferings large and small, assuring us that it has not all been for nothing." (p.322) Aldous Huxley has said that music expresses the inexpressible, and Victor Hugo agreed, adding that music expresses that on which it is impossible to be silent. So it is a communication, an expression, coming from the listener in response to the sounds created by the composer. And this expression is so deeply meaningful as to be essential. Beethoven alluded to this emotional component of the communication in this way: "Music should strike fire from the heart of man, and bring tears from the eyes of woman." And Martin Luther placed music next to Theology as a gift from God.

Heavy thoughts, these, and hard to reconcile with the rap coming from the lowrider in the next traffic lane. That music of rebellion, rage, and retribution, is only the latest in a long series of musical styles created to express the voices of the young, to tell of their hopes and needs when their viewpoints could not otherwise be heard. The less legitimate the person feels, the less hope he or she feels, the more their music will become a weapon in the generational war. Milder alienations breed milder music, but still shocking to those who are the status quo. And not just generation, but race, and other separations, have brought musical styles into existence to express the politically and socially inexpressible. Jazz and blues have played counterpoint to social change and political struggle for many years. Plato understood this long ago, and warned that the introduction of a new style of music "Must be shunned as imperiling the whole state."

But not just rage, not just frustration, are the stuff of music. Joy abounds there, too, and love, and passion, and sheer delight in living and moving. While music can certainly calm and charm, it also can excite and thrill. From the rocking chair to the dance floor, to the marching band, back to the rocking chair, and then, the funeral parade, music and motion are the dance of life, helping us feel, helping us be, human.

How best to live in this rhythm? Oliver Wendell Holmes said to "Take a music bath once or twice a week". I'd agree, for if you will, at least that often, just sit and listen closely, wonderful things will happen. Soon, you'll hear the structure of the piece, shortly after, you'll know which passages anticipate which others. Listen for the mood of the composer; ignore the words and listen to your own which arise to fit the sounds.

Then, if you can, spend some time, even if only a few minutes, each day singing or playing an instrument. Think of it as mastering a foreign language, and recognize that fluency in music will open doors to understanding that you cannot open any other way. When you have children, sing to them, no matter how weak you fear your voice may be. When they are old enough to select music you hate, try to be open minded enough to realize that rebellion is necessary, and this is a fairly safe type of war. If the lyrics are disturbing to you, that's an opportunity for some good conversation.

Finally, treat yourself to wonderful musical experiences. My mom took me every Christmas to hear Handel's Messiah at Union College. I would give anything to be able to go again with her, and I've never lost my love for that wonderful story. Go to symphony halls, go to rock concerts, go hear good musicians whenever you can, and thank them. Buy CDs that range all over the musical map, and listen to them several times in a row, deeper each time. Take a stab at writing music of your own. Learn to distinguish among the great composers. Learn the names of the songs loved by someone you love. Plunge in and revel in the beauty and excitement and fear and sorrow and peace that music can pull out of you, making your life make more sense. Music and math use and expand the same area of the brain, but math very rarely makes me weep with joy.

Workbook Questions:

1. What three musical pieces best express who you are? Would your best friend have the same list?
2. Why do you think younger people always seem to love music their parents dislike?
3. What steps can you take this week to build into your life more appreciation for the gifts of music?

Harmony

- The necessity of difference
- Harmony within leads to peace and trust
- Respect is essential to harmony with others

I'm an alto; how could I not write about harmony? When you were small, you used to give me strange looks in church when I sang something different from everyone else, but then, I guess you decided I wasn't doing any harm, because the strange looks stopped. I pointed out to you in the hymnal which notes others were singing and which I was singing, but I don't think that really registered then. I hope your singing in chorus has helped with the understanding of harmony.

It's a beautiful concept, the fitting together of unlike parts to make a more beautiful whole. Notice I said unlike parts. There's no harmony if everybody's singing the same note. There's no harmony if the painting is all one shade of blue. So we need unlike parts. Fortunately, there's no shortage of those. I'd like to explore three kinds of harmony with you; harmony within, harmony with others, and harmony with the larger world. If we can make some progress on these as individuals, our culture has a chance. If we can't the same old cycle of war and violence will be back for summer reruns, year after year after year.

The harmony within is called, more formally, congruence. That means that what you think, what you feel, and what you do are all the same sort of thing. If you know a little child and see him fall, you think he may be hurt. If you feel compassion, and you walk over to help him up, your thoughts, feelings, and actions are congruent, or harmonious. On the other hand, if you think he may be hurt, but you are busy and you don't acknowledge feeling any compassion, and you just go about your business without stopping to help, you're not being harmonious, and you will feel a kind of tension called guilt. To take another example, in business today there are laws against discrimination. If someone has an idea that they are superior to someone else because of their race or gender, and they really believe that and resent the other person's presence in the work group, their thoughts and feelings are congruent, but because of the law, they can't act to discriminate since that's illegal. So their action has to be accepting, even if their feelings and thoughts aren't. This leads to tension, and to suppressed rage, and to all kinds of problems in the workplace. The reason employers pay people like me to present training to such people is to bring about more harmony between thoughts, feelings, and actions, and harmony with the law as well. People who are harmonious within, or congruent, are comfortable with themselves. They won't be found saying or doing inconsistent things, so others rely on them and are comfortable with them, too. Mahatma Gandhi says that happiness is when what you think, what you say, and what you do are in harmony.

Harmony with others doesn't mean that we have to become like others, or that they have to become like us. Remember, we sing different notes to produce the sound of harmony. It means that we have to respect each other, and allow people to have their say and to be themselves. It means we spend some time learning how to communicate with respect, how to solve problems without violence or unfairness, how to support each other as we all learn. Martin Luther King said it well: If we do not learn to live together as sisters and brothers, we shall die together like fools. And it's true, the end result of lack of understanding is conflict; the end result of conflict is war, and the end result of war is death. It's a long road of personal growth to be able to contribute to this interpersonal harmony. You have to get rid of two thoughts that block it. One thought that must be left behind is the need to prove that you are right. Work at replacing it with a need to learn what is best for all concerned. The second thought that needs to be left behind is the desire to punish others. It is very hard, and very important, to turn toward the future and talk about what should be done next, rather than to look toward the past and talk about vengeance.

Finally, it's critical to work at bringing harmony to the third realm, the larger world. Albert Einstein saw a greatness of harmony in both art and science, and many others have commented on the harmony of the natural universe. Sit out alone a night and watch the stars, spend time listening to a symphony, contemplate a master painting, work out a difficult math equation. In all of these, there are lessons in harmony, lessons to take to heart. You will learn about resolving discord; you will learn about dominance and submission, you will learn about life. Your contemplation of these things won't make headlines, for harmony is a quiet joy, but you will learn lessons in reconciling opposites that will serve you well all your days.

Workbook Questions:

1. Are you usually able to act on your thoughts and feelings? How does that feel?
2. Have you noticed times when you felt you must act differently from your thoughts and feelings? How was that experience?
3. The need to be right feels natural. Why is it important to grow beyond that to produce harmony?

Truth

- Ways of knowing what is true vary, and all may be valid
- Evaluate why you believe in the things you believe in
- There are consequences for silencing your yearning for truth

Did you ever wonder why you have had to go to school at all? If you ask most kids, they'll either tell you that it's the law, or they wouldn't go, or they'll tell you that they want to get a good job when they grow up. Those are pretty good answers, but I think there are better reasons to exercise your mind and learn all those things you're learning. You, and everyone else who is studying something, are engaged in a search for truth, and you're learning how to learn, so you can keep searching for truth your whole life.

So how do you know when you've found it? How do you know when something is true? No, that's not a trick question, but a very important one. And it's one that people have very different answers to. In some cultures, the answer has to do with who told you something, what the source is. If it's somebody in authority, then that settles it, that's the truth. Well, you know that in the good old US of A, it doesn't work that way. If somebody in authority says something, at least eight people will be on the nightly news saying something different, and contradictory. Most of them will refer to their own experiences, or to history, which is just shared experience written from a particular perspective. Other people trust the latest research, which often does reveal new information, but will probably be outdated by still more research and information later on. Still others will refer to gut feelings, ethical standards, morality, or some other intangible standard for what's true and what's false. Confusing, isn't it? Sometimes it seems as though uncertainty is the only thing we can be sure of.

There is however, some solid ground to stand upon in our search. God's Word is truth, of course, but often it seems to come to us in code that's hard to decipher, and different people interpret it differently, which doesn't help. Where it is clear, though, it shines such as powerful beacon into our souls that we are faint with equal parts fear and gratitude. In these moments, we know the search for truth is worth every hour of studious effort and careful consideration.

For about ten years I worked as a professor and Dean at several colleges. I expected to find people busily tracking down truth in their fields, and I did find some of those. I also found a number of folks just as busily tracking down different, and lesser, things, like prestige, tenure, money, influence, and so on. In the consulting and training business I started later, I made a commitment to tell the truth as I knew it, and that made it easy to remember what I had said and where, for there were no games, no politics, and no giving in to whatever the boss in a certain organization wanted said. It was very satisfying, and I'm grateful for the experience. It was also very humbling, because I soon learned that the part of the truth I knew was a very small part indeed. That small part was, however, of help to a number of people, uplifting and encouraging them, and it's the sort of thing I hope to share with you in these letters.

Jesus said the truth will set you free. Just chasing after the truth sets you free, and getting it is unimaginably exhilarating. It's a rare and delightful thing, even if it isn't exactly what you were hoping to find. Partly, it's the search that's important, at least as much as the finding. Adrienne Rich, who tells the truth about women in her book *Of Woman Born*, says that the unconscious wants truth, and that it ceases to speak to those who want something else more than truth. She's talking about the loss of your own humanity when you silence your yearning for truth, and the inability later to recognize it even when you find it. Anais Nin, another searcher, said that there are very few who receive the truth, complete and staggering, by instant illumination. Most of them acquire it fragment by fragment. She also said that she doesn't tell the truth anymore to those who can't make use of it, but tells it mostly to herself, because it always changes her. And another woman who risked much for the truth, Elizabeth Cady Stanton, said, despite her risk, that truth is the only safe ground to stand upon. So these women giants of our history and our times tell us we must search, it will keep us sane and whole, it will be a great deal of work, and it's no use trying to discuss this with lots of other people. If it sounds difficult and lonely, that's right. Do you remember hearing of Diogenes, who searched and searched with his lantern for just one honest man, one truth seeker? Sometimes it seems as if there are few, or maybe none, left. And although Epictetus thought in ancient times that a lover and seeker of truth would be thought precious by his or her society, we know that the chances are just as good that the truth seeker will be locked up, or at least mocked.

But it's one of the most human and most divine tasks of life. Those who are called to search for truth, as those who are called to search for beauty, love, and justice, are gifted with an inner compass that helps in the seeking. You have to start by telling the truth to yourself about yourself. Then you have to develop your power of critical thinking, and in equal part, your power of intuition and caring. Truth does not favor the left brain or the right, but rather is harmonious with the whole person, ringing true, feeling right, and fitting and extending the best of prior knowing. Contemplation in the world, not apart from it, that's the path I would choose for you, and may your seeking be blessed, and your finding be a gift to you and those you love.

Workbook Questions:

1. How do you generally go about convincing yourself that something is true?
2. Do you know of anyone who has suffered for telling the truth? Should they have been silent?
3. Has your own understanding of truth changed as you've grown? Will it keep changing, do you think?

Friends

- The marvels of real friendship
- Friends will tell you painful truths if needed
- Maintaining friendships is a task many neglect

Cruz and I have been friends for thirty years. We've shared weddings, a divorce or two, sickness, funerals, fears, happiness, hope, our kids' and grandkids' problems and triumphs, job frustrations, big and little decisions, even, sometimes, clothes. We're stronger together, smarter together, more confident together, maybe even better-looking together. Sometimes we don't talk or email for months, but then, when we do, it's as if we never stopped. We know we can move in to each other's houses and lives whenever we need to, and we're working on trying to sort out the meaning of life in those irregular late night confessionals over a glass of wine. The other night I dreamed I was at her wedding, watching her—much younger, slender, lovely in a lavender lace fitted long sleeved top and a tiered lavender skirt with real flowers woven through lacy ribbons. Ever since, I've been wondering how to tell her that lavender really isn't her best color. And still she puts up with me!

Walking down the street here in Puerto Vallarta, young men shout mercenary greetings from every side: "Hey, my friend; you want a free dinner cruise?" As if listening to their boring, bullying timeshare presentation had anything to do with friendship! The real thing is so precious that I want to slap them for sullying the word.

The real thing—that marvelous, nurturing, satisfying harmony of souls, is already alive in your life. Each of you has found friends that you can share secrets with, friends who will back you up when you're under attack, friends that listen to your hopes and fears, friends that laugh at you and with you until you're laughing too. Lucky, lucky you.

George Eliot recommends animals as friends because they ask no questions and pass no criticisms. I don't agree—the best friends are those who will happily beat you up when you need it. Even though I dearly love animals, they're not the same thing as friends. Only a true friend will tell you when you're wrong; will criticize the action you're taking that isn't worthy of you, will ask the hard questions you'd prefer to avoid, will hold you to the high standard that makes you deserving of their love. And only a true friend will tell you when your skirt hem is caught up in your underpants in back, where you can't see it, but everyone else can.

Friendship begins with liking, and sometimes, with gratitude. Of all the people you see every day, only a few struck you as special enough that you could share what you really think, tell them where you hurt, tell them who you think is really cute. They didn't tell on you, so trust began to grow. They told you their secrets, and stood up for you when someone teased you. Maybe you'll be in chorus together, or on a team together. Maybe you'll get to go on a summer vacation together, or just hang around and talk. Maybe a few years from now you'll stand up to the cliques in high school or on a job together and survive to tell each other how scared you were. One or two of these friendships may survive the trials of college and adulthood, and new ones will grow as well. Take very good care of your friendships, and don't stop when the business of adulthood gets in the way. Far too many adults let their friendships wither away because they're too busy to call, too busy with babies, too busy with jobs, too busy with marriage and divorce, and then, when they need a friend, they have to look very hard to find one who's stuck it out through all the lonesome years.

You have to be a friend to have one, Emerson said. That I agree with. Take the time to make those phone calls, send those emails, issue those invitations, stick up for them, give them articles about things you know they're interested in, introduce them to people and places that will help them pursue their dreams, and listen, listen, listen. Then you can count yourself a good friend. When all the busyness is done, there will be a friend or two left to share the golden years with, to travel with, go to concerts with, and just sit and remember with.

The last argument I had with Cruz was because she hurt my feelings by purchasing property in another retirement town in Mexico, not near where I live. Never mind that she has the right to live anywhere she wants; never mind that my house is on the market and I'm moving anyway, I was furious. How could she not remember that we'd talked about sharing our late retirement years together, after all the men and kids in our lives were gone! Funny, how much that little joke we shared meant to me. She laughed at me and said she had only bought the property as an investment, so maybe our plan is still intact. Whether or not that works out, it underlined how very precious friends are, and how much I've come to count on those I hold dear. May both of you be blessed with a few most excellent, lifelong friends.

Workbook Questions:

1. List your three closest friends. Call, email, or write them this week to tell them why you appreciate them.
2. Do you have to be very similar to someone to be friends?
3. Have you ever quarreled with a friend, then made up, only to find the relationship stronger? Why do you think that is?

Being and Doing

- Untangle who you are from what you do
- Allow the spirit within you to develop
- Simple ways to help your spirit thrive

I grew up in upstate New York, which many residents considered to be part of New England. There was a great deal of pride in history there, and a strong Protestant flavor to public morality. We lived with a common understanding that work was good, that inactivity was evil laziness, and that God would reward those who worked diligently. Later on, I heard these ideas referred to as the Work Ethic, or the Protestant Ethic. By either name, my family danced to that song. Dad, particularly, spent long hours at work, and still longer hours, it seemed, in community service. Mom also worked, which was not typical of women then, and she cared for the house and served on church and PTA committees. We kids were expected to do well at school, be active in after school sports and interest clubs, volunteer at church, babysit when it was needed, and help around the house. If it's true that the devil finds work for idle hands, we sure were into prevention!

I was doing, doing, all the time—school, sports, homework, music lessons, and on and on. But sometimes there would be an hour or two for just being a kid, for fantasy adventures with cousins and friends, for building tree houses and lying under the pines, watching the clouds through the branches. It was during those times that my spirit began to form, I think, more so than the times when I was doing absolutely everything that was expected of me. In our culture, even where the Protestant Ethic doesn't hold sway, doing is still pretty much the measure of people's stature, and we always confuse what people do with who they are. I'd like to draw upon some experiences and some references to help you keep the two separate in your minds, and derive the benefits of both.

There's a real danger in confusing the two. People who over-identify with their jobs, that is, they think they are what they do, have a terrible time if they lose the job, or become ill and can no longer do it. They feel worthless, and they stand a real chance of loneliness and depression, because all their contacts and thoughts have had to do with the work. In some of my client organizations, there were a few people who had this soul-sickness unto death.

If someone asks you, "What are you going to be when you grow up?", I'd answer, at least in my mind, "Why, I'm going to be Kesla", or, "I'm going to be Kylie". Now, you might not want to say that out loud, at least not without a smile, for some people won't understand, but you already are somebody. Their real question is what do you think you want to do for work? There are no doubt several answers, at least, to that, and you can certainly say something like, "I'm not sure, but I'm interested in photography, or science, or horses, or whatever." Then, they will probably encourage you in the ways they know best about how to pursue those interests, and that's fine.

Although you're going to have to spend most of your waking hours for a very long time preparing to do some particular kind of work, and probably you'll spend still more hours learning about hobbies and sports that interest you, I'd like to encourage you to set aside some time for developing who you are, as well as what you might do. Who you are, being, in short, has to do with your character, your essence, your spirit. Those things are in danger of being neglected in our work-oriented culture, but they are, ultimately, vastly more important.

To develop the spirit within you, read inspirational things, pray and meditate quietly, be still and listen for guidance. Fill your eyes and mind with beautiful things, especially from nature, fill your ears with both lovely silence and grand music, and move slowly, thoughtfully, within a quiet place of contemplation. Then, run like the wind until you can move no more, to test and extend your limits. Listen to moving water, listen to birds calling, feel gentle breezes, and spend time just looking at the stars. These disciplines will calm you, allowing your nature to become all that it can be. Seek out people of good heart and wise mind for guidance, and test what they tell you against your own developing understanding of truth. Hold all your ideas gently, being ready to expand them as new understanding comes to you. Love visibly and selflessly, in small and large ways, daily. Hold yourself to the highest standards, but allow others to choose their own goals and means.

That is the you that is created, that is the you that is loved, and that is the you that leaves a legacy upon this earth in the hearts and minds of those that know you. It's your center, and it needs to be pure, disciplined, and free to take the shape of its destiny, to spin and breathe and be formed, just as a potter shapes the clay. When I worked and lived as a potter, I read M.C. Richards' book *Centering*, which poetically describes the parallels between the dawn of beauty from the clay and the dawn of consciousness from the person's spirit.

This you that is becoming into being is the tool you have to find, live, and speak the truth. *The Tao of Leadership* says "The leader teaches more through being than through doing . . . The leader who knows how to be still and feel deeply will probably be effective." (P.45) In our culture it's often said this way, "Who you are shouts so loudly that I can't hear what you're saying". By paying attention to who you are, you can be effective in all aspects of your life, and feel a satisfaction in living that is out of reach for those who are following a formula of frantic activity. As Chin-Ning Chu says in *Do Less, Achieve More*, "When I am totally on purpose, I find that I attract the specific, beneficial phone calls that tend to help me expedite the completion of my immediate task . . ." That's a small, but telling, example of how much more smoothly life proceeds when the focus is on being, rather than on doing. The same author points out how thriving grows from focusing on duty, risk, and exhilaration, rather than on fear. May your spirits thrive as you explore both who you are and what you will do in this world.

Workbook Questions:

1. Write four things you can do. Write four words that describe who you are. Evaluate.
2. Think of someone you admire. Why? Do you respect what they can do, or who they are?
3. Which of the two, being and doing, contributes more to leadership ability? Why?

Tortugas

- Greed destroys, far more than we seem to know
- Small actions, taken by many, make a substantial difference
- Environment issues are the business of life for all of us

Do you remember the Christmas when you came to visit us in Mexico? On the first night, since you were still on California time, we stayed up late to help rescue baby turtles at the beach. I seem to recall, Kesla, that you were disgusted with your "too-slow" turtle, but both of you loved seeing them all head for the waves, and then you headed for the waves, too, a little further up the beach.

It's too bad the lecture was all in Spanish, and we didn't understand enough to learn the details about these particular turtles, or what their survival chances would have been without a little help from their friends. Survival—that's what it was all about, and we probably did make a difference, at least for those few turtles. And when you think that each evening during the egg-hatching season, hundreds of people line up along the beach of this beautiful bay to wish the baby turtles well and to give them a hand getting started in life, maybe we were doing some good, after all. We were helping to correct the balance, working to undo some of the damage our greedy species has done.

It may seem odd to you that I call us greedy, but we are. Especially those of us from the US, who consume much more than our share of the world's resources, and don't seem to be willing to cut back very much to make it possible for others to thrive. We've forgotten that our job is to be stewards of the earth and its resources, to take such good care of it that we leave it better for our having been here.

You grew up with recycling, and once a year Earth Day provides your teachers a special opportunity to instruct you in the wise use of earth's resources. It seems like a normal, minor responsibility to you, and it may surprise you to learn that many people don't see it that way in the US, or in other places. I was already an adult when the first Earth Day happened. One of my artist friends made a beautiful woodcut to commemorate that very significant event, and I still have it in a place of honor. But when I lived in Ethiopia, and later in Mexico, I learned that often the recycling that is done is just to get the most use from scarce resources, because that's what poverty dictates. Fortunately, a number of visionary people are spreading the word that it's very important for everyone to be careful with the resources of our beautiful natural world. The turtle rescue programs are a part of that wisdom.

And sometimes the good guys win. Just last year the news was been full of a thought-to-be-extinct bird, the Ivory-billed woodpecker, now found in an eastern Arkansas refuge. It's worth celebrating when something beautiful is rediscovered, somehow having survived in spite of us.

There was a time when people in the US all thought about being careful, about conservation. They were thinking finances, not wildlife, but it's all part of the same mind-set. My grandmother Conger, who lived through the Great Depression, had a saying: "Use it up, wear it out, make it do, do without". I hated that saying then, because I was just learning that I could earn a little money, save it, and buy things I wanted. The idea of doing without, or re-using something old, was just not in my plans! Now, I feel the truth of her words, even though it's still wonderful to save for something really special and be able to get it.

You're just beginning to think about jobs and careers. Soon you will be earning a little money in part-time odd jobs. It will be easy for you to grow wants so much faster than your ability to earn, especially at first. This note is Grandma's way of asking you to do some careful thinking, so that you can enjoy your new power responsibly, without wasting resources—yours or the earth's.

Here are a few suggestions. Before you throw something away, take another look—can it be re-used, traded, sold, given away, or refurbished into something useful? Before you make a large purchase, can you ask the seller to hold it overnight while you think some more about whether you really need it? With regard to clothes, consider the European way of doing things—which, by the way, your Dad seems to have come by quite all on his own. They prefer to have a few high quality things rather than a lot of lower-quality things that will wear out and look shabby very soon. Can you recycle as much as possible yourself, and encourage others—at school, at work later on, and in your community—to do the same? Can you learn to live on less than you earn and to set aside some? Can you learn to fix things, at least some things, so there's less to throw away?

That's what we were doing with those cute baby turtles—fixing things. Hopefully, we won't be like that "too-slow" turtle, but our responsible actions will be in time to make a difference. Your children will be the judges of whether we succeeded or failed in the long run. I'd like those children—my great-grandchildren—to be proud of us.

Workbook Questions:

1. What are the two most significant resource issues in your opinion? Will individual effort make a difference in these issues?
2. Why do you think recycling is important?
3. How can we educate ourselves to be more sensitive to the earth and its other inhabitants?

Why Art?

- A brief primer on the visual arts
- How value is determined
- Why do we respond to art as we do?

There are lots of different arts—music, dance, visual arts, performance art, and so on, but what most people think of as art, are pictures on museum walls, and maybe those big sculptures outside in cities where there could have been perfectly good parking places instead. Lots of people think it's foolish, or mysterious, and some people, like me, love it more than they can bear. I'd like to take some of the mystery out of visual art that doesn't need to be there, and remind you of some of the mystery that has to be there.

First, forgive me for taking you through some basics you probably already know. Visual art is generally two or three dimensional, that is, flat or "in the round". There's an in-between type, called relief, which is flat only on the back. In all art, the word *medium* refers to the material the artist uses to make the art, whether it's marble, clay, oil paint, or sawdust. Mixed media means the artist got a little wild and used more than one kind of material to make the art. Pieces of art can be tiny miniatures or as large as buildings. In order for a piece of work to be art, rather than practice, it should show both creativity and craftsmanship—a new vision, presented well.

Some of the monetary value of art comes from its rarity. If the artist is well known and respected, and there's only one copy in the world of some piece of art made by him or her, it's very costly, especially if the artist is no longer producing. Usually only museums or millionaires can own a piece like that. Many artists, however, make multiple copies of their work, either casting a number of sculptures just alike, or printing more than one copy of their two-dimensional artwork. The techniques used might be silkscreen, lithography, etching, or other types of printing. As a rule these are much less expensive than the one-of-a-kind originals. Just to confuse everybody, the name for photographically produced copies of original artwork is also prints, and that type generally is not nearly as valuable as the originals. Most of the artwork you've seen in my collection is original prints; there may be as many as one hundred pieces similar to each of them in the world. Those terms and mechanics will, I hope, help you understand what art is made of and how it's made.

But far more interesting and curious are the questions of why the artist made it, and what his or her purpose was. Why do people respond as they do, and why are there such different tastes in art? Why do I stand weeping, immobilized before a Rothko in the San Francisco Museum of Modern Art, while Bob is anxious to get on to the café? The answers to those kinds of questions are much more useful for living a full life than knowing that you can walk around a sculpture, but not around a painting.

When we used to go to the Children's Museum and you put on smocks and painted and painted, there was a freedom and a pleasure in that expression, and some of the results were delightful to look at. A serious artist feels some of that same freedom, but also has the training or experience to know about line, proportion, light and shadow, color, shape and composition. All those are part of the how, but the why is something different. Listen to some of the reasoning artists give to explain why they create. Picasso said, art is a lie which makes us see the truth. Chagall said, art seems to me to be a state of soul more than anything else. Bertold Brecht said that art is not a mirror held up to reality, but a hammer with which to shape it. Jean Dubuffet said, art addresses itself to the mind, and not to the eyes. Robert Henri said, a work of art is the trace of a magnificent struggle. The sculptor Giacometti said that basically, he no longer worked for anything but the sensation he has while working. A lie, a struggle, hammering out a new reality, a state of soul, but so compelling that nothing else could be substituted, no other activity yield the satisfaction of creating art. Trevor Bell sums it all up this way: "Art condenses the experience we all have as human beings, and, by forming it, makes it significant . . . Basically art is an affirmation of life".

Beyond affirmation, though, there is a quality of redemption for the viewer, the other half of the artist's conversation. Art does something to the viewer; it makes that person's knowledge and self-knowledge both deeper and more real. As an outward symbol of the interior life we all have, but usually don't share, art communicates one soul's fear and fire to another. We approach a work of art with our intelligence, yes, but also with our heart, wanting to be inspired, to grow in understanding. In the best of circumstances, our chaos is reduced, and we are able to think more subtly and feel more nobly for having communed with the artist's very being through his or her expression. To put it simply, if we will quiet ourselves and let the art speak to us, we will grow, and we will become more human.

We have a piece of art in the living room by Helen Frankenthaler. It's called Causeway, which means a raised path across low, wet ground. It's grey on the sides, pink in the center, full of subtle colorations and delightful shapes, and I love it. I see on the side with clean edges to the colors, Bob's way of thinking, in mostly black and white. On the side with the blurred edges, I see my tendency to see many different sides to an issue. The lines across, joining the two, for us stand for our love, tolerance, and regard for one another. The artist's idea of bridging has become, in our interaction with the artwork, a symbol of the work we do every day to understand each other. When you bring yourself to the art, as we do to this, there's an interchange, and you leave the encounter better. Maybe that's why I can never resist an art show—there's so much growing to do!

Workbook Questions:

1. What does it mean to "bring yourself to the art"? How would you do that?
2. Is art that disturbs, or shocks, still art?
3. What is your favorite piece of art? What does it mean to you?

Having It All

- Fulfillment in work and love
- Pacing yourself in the stages of a full and meaningful life
- Secrets of satisfaction from youth to retirement

I read today—I'd forgotten—that Johann Sebastian Bach not only produced 1000 works of music in his life, works which have long set the standard for others—but he also fathered 21 children, some of whom were also highly gifted composers. Sigmund Freud, who was not the father of many children, but was the father of psychology, said that all we have in this life is work and love. Those are the only places where we can make a difference, leave our mark. If he's right, and I suspect he is, then Bach did a fine job of having it all, or at least, of doing it all!

You might not know that "having it all" is kind of a code phrase that women of my generation took as a goal—to be equal with men in careers (a new thought then), and to raise bright, good and caring children, have a lovely home, and make a contribution to the community. Many, many women made enormous sacrifices to open opportunities for others, especially in jobs that used to hire or promote only men.

By the time my daughters' generation came along and started to go to work, it was more natural that they expect the same challenges, the same opportunity, and the same pay as men with similar talent and education. But, a funny thing happened—they were not so likely to talk about wanting to "have it all". Maybe it's just that they don't have anything to prove, since no one feels they are less than competent. Or, maybe it's that they saw the price tag for having it all, and choose to pass. You know, I can understand that. After a few decades of trying, and often succeeding, in having it all, I'm far more likely to believe now that a better motto is: "You can have it all, just not all at once."

What that means to me is to take advantage of the natural stages of life and the changes in focus that they bring, along with changing energy levels. Taking Freud's advice about creating life's meaning in the arenas of love and work, we can look for wisdom in the strategies of balance and timing. For example, right now your job is to grow in wisdom and stature, to build the best foundation you can of a strong healthy body and a strong healthy mind. A little later, you'll seriously begin the process of selection—choosing a career for at least the first few years of your working life, and choosing a mate for hopefully far longer than that. Neither can be rushed, and false starts, mistakes, are just part of the learning process. At the same time, you'll begin to widen your experience in the world, to understand more about your culture and others, to start to develop a style that's your own, and to find satisfying ways to reach out to others. You'll begin to be more sure of who you are.

Treasure those years of thoughtful first steps, for soon the dizzying rush of adulthood will demand all your strength, time, and resources. To advance in a career you must dedicate yourself to long hours. To build a solid marriage, you must find time to work at it. To establish a warm and welcoming home it's necessary to learn about cooking, decorating, furnishing, and many other arts. To serve the community, it's important to join organizations that add your strength to that of others to solve difficult problems. Just as you think that's all anyone could possibly do, a parent becomes ill, and a child, or another child, is born, and your priorities shift again.

I've often commented in training sessions that adults are notoriously poor at friendships, just because they are so overwhelmed with other responsibilities. Friends can provide wonderful support during this period, so please don't neglect them.

A little later, you'll feel strong financial demands—home mortgages, college funds for the kids, medical bills perhaps, and this will keep you working for career moves that pay a little better. It feels like the pressure will never ease, and then, all of a sudden, it does, with retirement. There may not be enough money for even all the basics at this stage, but there is definitely more time, and if you've taken good care of your body, enough energy to use the time productively. There's an urge at this life stage called Generativity, which several psychologists have written about. It's the desire to pass along what you've learned about life, so the next generation might have things a bit easier. That's why you're getting these letters, of course. Others express the urge through charitable work, making things better for others in that way. This wonderful, satisfying stage can last a long time. I just read that a recent national poet laureate was still working and writing at 100.

This is also a time for reflection, for summing up what the value of your life has been. Martin Seligman's book, Authentic Happiness, talks about this, and it's a nice way to think about the question of having it all. Roughly put, he says that the good life maximizes pleasure, the full life maximizes gratification, and the meaningful life maximizes service. I wish for you, more than you'll ever imagine, good, full, and meaningful lives, having it all, and the gift of patience that will help you pace yourselves. You can, and will, I'm sure, have it all, but probably not all at once.

Workbook Questions:

1. For your own life right now, how would you define "having it all"?
2. Why is service thought to be more meaningful than pleasure?
3. Do you think there is a "best" stage of life?

Zest

- Replace the zombie lifestyle with a zestful life
- Enthusiasm makes the best memories
- A few simple safeguards

The dictionary says that zest is the peel of a fruit, like a lemon. Well, we know what that tastes like! I think it's a far, far better thing than that—it's the stuff that makes life worth living, the stuff that lifts anything out of the ordinary and turns it into a wild, crazy, uninhibited frolic. You see people all the time who never heard of it—they are the zombies just going through the motions of life. They talk in monotones, look bored, sigh a lot, and you want to poke them to see if they're alive. Why would anyone take life at idle speed? Probably fear, and maybe an overdose of common sense. You know, the kind that says, don't run, you could fall; don't speak to that stranger, she might be nasty; don't raise your hand, your answer might be wrong. If we listened to that voice, we'd be safe all right, but safe for what? Living with a layer of bubble wrap all around to protect us is not really living at all. You can't see much through it, and you can't taste or smell or feel anything.

Every day you make choices either to go through the motions, or to add that extra bit of energy, attention, and little touch of passion that makes everything you do a little more exciting, a little more alive. Sure, you get bruises that way, and heartbreak, too, but you never doubt that you are alive, and you don't feel as if you're waiting for something to begin—it's already here. Ask someone what their favorite memory is, and I'll bet you anything that the memory that brings a smile, and maybe a tear, will be of something done at full tilt, of dancing to life's music, not sitting on the sidelines. It's a delicate balance, to be sure, to avoid the madness of rushing full speed into disaster, and yet to be raw, open, and ready for all that life has to offer. If there's a neat formula, I don't know it, but I do want to share a few tips with you.

First, keep your limits and safeguards very simple. If something is illegal, and you can't justify it on moral grounds, don't do it. If something is life-threatening, and you don't have the skill to dare it anyway, don't do it. If something will cause great harm to others, don't do it. If something will break the bank, and make you dependent on others for the rest of your life, don't do it. That's it. Otherwise, the world is yours to take on, wrestle with, and love. Whenever an opportunity comes along, take it. When life asks if you can do something, say "Sure!". And so I've gotten to travel the world, get an education, teach, write, make art, make love, make music, raise children, learn languages, share my soul with strangers, learn about others' deepest hopes and fears, embrace the beauty of the world, and cook a mean lasagna. And I can't wait to see what's next!

Second, keep your hunger for experience very much in your awareness. Once a week or so, try a food you've never eaten before. When you go to the mall, stop in a store and listen to a CD by a group you've never heard of, maybe one from Asia or Africa. Walk home by a slightly different route once in awhile. Watch a TV show in Spanish. Wear a color you thought you didn't like, and see what your friends say. Sing something, grow something, cook something, write something, draw something, build something. Join a new club or after-school sport. Ask lots of questions, and listen to the answers. Think about it all, keep the things that make you feel stronger, smarter, more hopeful, curious for more. Discard the rest, or save those for another try later on.

Third, crank up the intensity. That doesn't necessarily mean louder and brighter, but it might. Mostly, it means whatever you're doing right now, pay attention to it, focus on it, put your whole self into it. You get out of most things whatever you put into them. Seems obvious, so why not take advantage of that rule and give it all you've got? Keep a list of "bests", and ask others for their choices for "bests"—best chocolate ice cream, best sunset, best Christmas carol, best vacation, best everything. A little more quietly, keep a list of worsts—worst cookies you ever made, worst fight with your sister, worst day of the year, and so forth. Zest is mostly, but not all, about the good stuff. It's about wringing the most from every experience; the most learning, the most feeling, the most growth.

Fourth, keep falling in love with life. In my opinion, it's a crime to go through life in a state of "like", pleasant but not passionate. What a waste of human feeling, potential, and talent. If you're feeling a little bored and discouraged, do something adventurous. Adventure will put you in the right frame of mind, so never turn it down. Go into each day with an attitude of expectation; knowing something wonderful is about to happen, and you're about to meet some fascinating people. Your expectation radiates a kind of energy that actually brings these things to you. Whether you're expecting something terrific or something terrible, you're more likely to get exactly what you expect than its opposite. It has to do with your body language and its effect on others. So why not make that rule work in your favor, too?

Here in Mexico, the expression for "I like" is "Me gusto!" That's it exactly, gusto. In English, the word means hearty enjoyment, keen relish, delight. What's not to like? Or, more to the point, what's not to love?

Workbook Questions:

1. Write about a time when you lived "at full throttle". Was it worth it?
2. What fears are keeping you from being more adventurous? What safeguards might help?
3. Describe a perfect day. Is it more active and involved, or more quiet and passive? Why?

Bibliography

Abbott, Linda M.C. *Fresno, Valley of Abundance*. Fresno, Ca. Fresno City and County Chamber of Commerce, 1989.

Alessandra, Anthony J., Tony Alessandra, and Michael J. O'Connor. *The Platinum Rule*. 1998.

Brehony, Kathleen A. *Ordinary Grace*. New York, Riverhead Books, 1999.

Chin-Ning Chu. *Do Less, Achieve More*. New York, Regan, 1998.

Covey, Stephen R., A. Roger Merrill, and Rebecca R. Merrill, *First Things First Every Day*. New York, Simon & Schuster, 1997.

Goleman, Daniel. *Working with Emotional Intelligence*. New York, Bantam Books, 1998.

Gray, John. *Men are From Mars, Women are From Venus*. New York HarperCollins, 1992.

Heider, John. *The Tao of Leadership*. New York, Bantam Books, 1985.

Holy Bible, The. King James Version. Cleveland and New York, The World Publishing Co., n.d.

Horn, Sam. *Tongue Fu!* New York, St. Martin's Griffin, 1996.

Jourdain, Robert. *Music, The Brain, and Ecstasy*. New York, William Morrow and Company, Inc., 1997.

Leman, Dr. Kevin, *The Birth Order Book*. Old Tappan, New Jersey, Fleming H. Revell Company, 1985.

Moss, Barbara Robinette. *Change Me Into Zeus's Daughter.* New York Simon & Schuster, 2000.

O'Connor, Richard. *Undoing Depression.* Boston, Little, Brown and Company, 1997.

Offer, Daniel, M.D., Eric Ostrov, J.D., PhD., Kenneth I. Howard, PhD, and Robert Atkinson, PhD. *The Teenage World: Adolescents' Self-Image in Ten Countries.* New York, Plenum Medical Book Company, 1988.

Peck, M. Scott. The Road Less Traveled. New York, Simon and Schuster, 1979.

Rich, Adrienne. *Of Woman Born.* New York, W.W. Norton & Company Inc. 1976.

Richards, M.C. *Centering.* Middletown, Connecticut, Wesleyan University Press, 1964.

Seligman, Martin, PhD., *Authentic Happiness.* New York, Free Press, 2002

Tannen, Deborah. *You Just Don't Understand.* New York, Ballentine Books, 1990.

The Quotable Woman. Vol.1. Elaine Partnow, Ed. Los Angeles, Pinnacle Books, 1977.

Tyler, Forrest B. *Cultures, Communities, Competence, and Change.* New York, Kluwer Academic/Plenum Publishers, 2001.

Valuing Diversity. Lewis Brown Griggs and Lente-Louise Louw, eds. New York, McGraw-Hill, 1995.

Webster's New Universal Unabridged dictionary. New York, Random House Value Publishing Inc., 1996.